TALES OF THE
GREAT WESTERN RAILWAY

Informal recollections of a near-lifetime's association with the line

O. S. Nock
BSc, CEng, FICE, FIMechE
Past-President IRSE

DAVID & CHARLES
Newton Abbot   London   North Pomfret (Vt)

British Library Cataloguing in Publication Data
Nock, O. S.
  Tales of the Great Western Railway.
  1. Great Western Railway – History
  I. Title
  385′.0942   HE3020.G8
  ISBN 0–7153–8347–7

Photoset in Plantin by
Northern Phototypesetting Co, Bolton
and printed in Great Britain by
Redwood Burn Ltd, Trowbridge, Wilts
for David & Charles (Publishers) Limited
Brunel House, Newton Abbot, Devon

Published in the United States of America
by David & Charles Inc
North Pomfret, Vermont 05053, USA

Contents

Preface   4

1   Reading in Broad Gauge days   6

2   Sir Felix Pole: Some Recollections   19

3   On Slip Coaches, Brakes, and Bearings   34

4   Seven Ages of GWR Coaches   46

5   Signals and Signalling Men   60

6   Swindon: The Churchward Era   73

7   GWR and the Press: J. A. Kay   87

8   The Wivelscombe Rock Fall   99

9   The Locomotive Department under Hawksworth   109

10 Control – the GW way   124

11 Special trains and 'Trip'   138

12 High Drama on the Cambrian   154

13 The Great Western Tradition and its Influence   161
    Index   175

Preface

The idea of this book grew from a dinner party that David Thomas and I, and our wives, enjoyed on a cold winter's night, in Bath. Cosily ensconced we were all talking about anything but business, but inevitably, I suppose, we got on to railways, and from time to time to the approaching sesquicentenary of the Great Western Railway. Having lived on the line for 65 out of my present span of years it was natural enough for me to gossip about this and that. But for all my experience, and the hundred or so books I have written about railways I never seemed to have learned how dangerous it is to reminisce in the hearing of a publisher. And sure enough before that evening was ending David said: 'You ought to put some of the things you've been talking about tonight into a book – not a definitive history, but something quite informal, like *Tales of the GWR*.'

Now that was all very well! I have already written 17 books entirely confined to the Great Western Railway, its history, its locomotives and train services, not to mention extensive references to it in more general works, and in many of the 264 articles on 'Locomotive Practice and Performance' that I contributed to *The Railway Magazine*. But the old railways of Britain all had an aura of their own – none more so than the Great Western – and in this latter case an aura that has survived nationalisation, and a determined implanting by the 'Centre' of alien influences intended to break up the old traditions. It has nevertheless been amusing to see how, with one exception, the implantees have fallen so completely under the spell as to earn comments from the natives that they had become 'more GW than any of us'. And here am I, despite earlier protestations that I had played myself out, settling into my stride for yet another book, with a story that I hope will evoke memories and express grateful thanks to many Great Western men who have given generously of their time and their continued friendship to help me with many previous books, and who are remembered now as much for their vibrant personalities as for their professional achievement, great as much of it unquestionably was. No less am I indebted to those who at various times since 1948 have become 'naturalised-GW' to the great advantage of continued good railroading in the West Country.

O. S. Nock

1
Reading in Broad Gauge days

Rather more than 40 years ago, correspondence with a man named Charles Doncaster ripened into a delightful pen friendship. It was an unusual name to have any connection with the Great Western Railway, but for the moment that is apart from the point. He was a locomotive photographer, but of an unusual kind and truly rare vintage, and what first brought us together, through the post, was his familiarity and love of the Midland Railway in the north country, under whose spell I myself had fallen in my school days at Giggleswick. Doncaster had been taking photographs of Midland engines before I was born, and then in those drab, anxious, blitz-torn days of the 1940–1 winter an opportunity came to meet him personally. Westinghouse business took me to Sheffield, where I discovered that he was Chairman of a very old established steel firm, Daniel Doncaster & Co. In the quiet pleasance of his home topics of conversation switched quickly, and surprisingly to the Great Western.

Now I have the clearest recollections of the GWR in the environs of Reading in the years 1907 to 1916, but here, in 1941, within the blacked-out windows of that country home near Sheffield, I was listening enthralled to the reminiscences of a man who was sent to a boarding school in Reading two years *before* the final 1892 abolition of the broad gauge! He was there for seven years, and his recollections of that time, of his term-end journeys between Reading and Sheffield, and his remarkably comprehensive lineside observations were all the more interesting and compelling to me, having seen trains from the same viewpoints at a period only about 15 years later. But as he talked, and produced album after album of old photographs I could not help reflecting upon the phenomenal change that had come over the Great Western scene in that relatively short period. By the time war came in 1914, Churchward had 77 two-cylinder and 61 four-cylinder 4–6–0s at work, enough

6

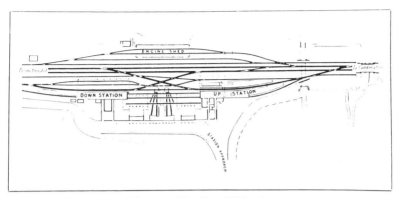

Diagram of Reading Old Station

to handle all the West of England, Bristol, and South Wales expresses passing through Reading. Only the Worcester trains lay outside this envelope, whereas when Doncaster's school days were done there was only an occasional Badminton class 4–4–0 to vary the otherwise interminable procession of single-wheelers.

From what Charles Doncaster told me on that first visit, and in the fascinating correspondence and further contacts that followed, it was evident that the youthful engine spotters of 1890, smartly attired in their school caps, were not unwelcome in the precincts of what was known at that time as Reading Central station. In the 1890s the track layout and platform arrangement was not quite the same as originally designed by Brunel when the line was first built, for in Doncaster's schooldays it consisted of one very long platform at which all trains stopping at Reading, both eastbound and westbound, were accommodated. Non-stopping trains had a clear run through, outside. From the traffic working point of view, as business developed, it could not have been worse, with the connections from the through lines intersecting everything else in reaching that one long platform. Originally, the down and up sections of the station were not connected. The only other difference that Doncaster and his school friends saw from the days of Brunel was the interposing of the mixed gauge, which made the track work even more complicated. But from a spotter's point of view that immensely long platform was ideal. It was a grandstand from which the passing trains on the through lines could be seen to the greatest advantage, because at both ends the platform extended far beyond the overall roof.

7

That the original layout could be an unmitigated nuisance was realised before the station had long been in operation, and as early as 1853 Brunel himself sketched out two alternative proposals for a revised layout. In both of these the single long platform concept is abandoned. In the first, instead of taking all eastbound trains right across the layout to the down side a separate platform was proposed on the opposite side, served by a loop off the up main line; but then, evidently realising the inconvenience of this from the passenger viewpoint he produced the second proposal. Neither scheme was adopted, and the only variation from the original layout, and that no more than a makeshift, was when mixed gauge was first introduced in the 1860s. It was evidently considered quite infra dig to accommodate standard gauge trains in the main station, and two narrow wooden platforms out in the open were built for these trains, appropriately inconvenient for passenger access! They had disappeared when Doncaster was at school in Reading. By that time, of course, the important expresses to Birmingham, Chester, and Birkenhead were standard gauge.

The widening of the main line to provide four tracks throughout from Paddington to Didcot was in full swing even before the final conversion of the gauge, in 1892. Heavy engineering work was in progress at the west end of Sonning cutting. The new retaining walls in the deepest part of the cutting were finished before the gauge conversion, but the two mixed gauge tracks, then carrying all traffic, were still in the centre, and by May 1892 only one relief line in standard gauge had been laid in on the north side, and used principally by works trains. When work was completed the new down main line was taken through the narrow space between the south pillar of the Bath Road bridge and the retaining wall, but the alignment was later changed to put three tracks through the centre arch. Even in those days it was a favourite place for watching trains, but after the four-track system was complete, and Reading station rebuilt, it was impossible to photograph down expresses in the most picturesque part of the cutting because they were immediately beneath the high retaining wall. A photograph taken from the parapet of the Bath Road bridge, and reproduced in *The Railway Magazine* in January 1917, shows the situation clearly.

While the broad gauge was still in existence, and the only two running lines were in the middle of the already widened cutting, the situation was ideal until late afternoon, when the sun had moved round to an almost head-on position for a down train. And

8

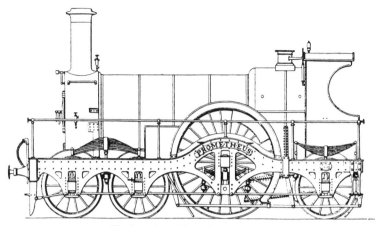

Final version of broad gauge 4–2–2s

what a feast of things came westwards through that cutting! The principal expresses were still hauled by the magnificent Gooch 8ft singles. A present-day reader may well imagine how positively transported I felt on that winter's night in 1941, talking to a man who had seen those legendary locomotives in action, and had been standing by when his older friends photographed them. It was not until 1894 that he had his own first camera. Then there would come one of those extraordinary ugly convertible 2–2–2s. Listening to Doncaster's recollections, I can well believe how incredibly wrong they looked, with those great 7ft 8in driving wheels stuck far out on each side of the boiler, with nothing but a top covering to shield them. I should imagine they were the only engines on which the driver, going forward to oil the motion, could pass *between* the driving wheel and the boiler! Each wheel had to be moved 1ft 2in inwards when the gauge conversion was made.

The transformation of these engines, after 1892, was unbelieveable. Actually, only eight of them were built on the convertible principle, Nos 3021–3028, between April and August 1891, and in that condition they were not named. But at the end of 1891 construction of more began, in the form they had been designed for the standard gauge, still as 2–2–2s. For this wheel arrangement they were long and heavy engines, graceful, and liberally adorned with polished brass and copper-work; after the conversion of the gauge in 1892 there were enough to take over the entire express passenger service between Paddington, Bristol and Newton Abbot. From all accounts, and it is surprising what home

9

truths could be learned by schoolboys gossiping with friendly enginemen, these beautiful engines in their 2–2–2 days were not very good riders. They had 19 tons on the driving axle, but only $13\frac{1}{4}$ on the leading and 12 tons on the trailing axle, and they tended to see-saw. In addition, although they were by no means the longest six-wheelers to have a fixed wheelbase the leading axle-boxes were given a lateral play of 2in. Unsteadiness from one cause or another led to engine No 3021 *Wigmore Castle* going off the road in Box Tunnel of all places in 1893. As a result, all 30 of the engines built as 2–2–2s were rebuilt with leading bogies, and became one of the classic locomotive beauties of all time.

The schoolboy photographers of that era with cumbersome box-type cameras having a primitive form of shutter release of distinctly erratic performance had much to record besides main line express locomotives. There were the signals, for example. To some eyes a semaphore signal was a signal and that was all there was to it; but, at that time, Great Western apparatus was at a most interesting and transitory stage. As on so many railways in Victorian times the semaphores worked in a slot in the post, originating from the time when the arm hanging vertically down disappeared entirely to give the all-right indication. On the many slotted posts that remained in the early 1890s the arm in a diagonal position was the clear signal, but the lamp was fixed about 4ft or 5ft lower down the post. Photographs taken around Reading showed some of the more modern type semaphores fixed outside the post, but still with the separate lamp. At that time white was the all-right indication at night time, and there were none of the modern optical refinements for giving a pure white light, by means of the 'lunar white' type of stepped lens. When the semaphore was moved to the all-right position the co-acting spectacle glass moved completely clear of the lamp, and the indication was merely that of the oil-lamp flame, projected through the simple bulls-eye lens of the lamp itself. There can have been few extraneous lights in the station yards or the adjoining streets and houses to confuse the light-display presented to an engine driver!

The first sign of a change was in the introduction, about 1890, of a better proportioned semaphore, in which the spectacle glass was incorporated in the arm itself. Again however the design was peculiar. One of Doncaster's school friends, venturing just beyond the London end of the up platform to photograph a down non-stopping broad gauge express approaching at full speed secured not only a fine picture of one of the Gooch 8ft singles but an interesting assortment of signals. In the background the down line bracket home had semaphores of the old type, with separate lamps, but prominent in the immediate foreground was an obviously new signal controlling the outlet from the up main line platform, which ran diagonally across the down main line to reach the up through line. That new signal, while still having no more than a single glass had a huge roundel of a diameter quite 50 per cent greater than the width of the semaphore blade itself. The decision to adopt green as the all-right signal was taken in 1895, but from all accounts it was several years before the change was completed. Originally green had been the caution indication.

However splendid a grandstand that single long platform might have been for viewing the non-stopping trains as they passed through, rarely at more than about 55mph, there was a far greater attraction on the north side. When Brunel laid out the design of the original station he did what many early railways also did, and put the engine sheds abreast of the station itself. The position can be seen from the sketch map, and to those young enthusiasts the activities at the sheds were tantalisingly near, and in fairly good view from the station platform, but with far too many incidental obstructions to make any form of photography practicable. Furthermore, the interests of those young enthusiasts extended far beyond the lordly glamour of the Gooch eight-footers, wheeling the few broad gauge expresses to the West. Well it might, because in 1890–1 everything else that came into Reading was standard, or what was then called 'narrow' gauge on the GWR, with an unbelievably great variety of tender and tank engines. How access to that shed was eventually obtained was a heart warming story.

It was no more than natural for the be-capped young gentlemen and their cameras to foregather at the country end of that long platform, for there, almost infalliably, was a handsomely groomed 2–4–0 express engine, No 2210, standing pilot. She was one of a class built at Swindon in 1882, but subsequently modernised to some extent, and having $17\frac{1}{2}$in by 24in cylinders, 6ft 6in coupled wheels and a domed boiler. She might appropriately have been named *Micawber*, for she stood there for day after day, week after week, waiting for a job to turn up — which it hardly ever did. Whether she ever went away on a secret errand in the dead of night was not vouchsafed to Doncaster and his friends; the crews who manned it during the day seemed glad of some youthful company. The

11

number of photographs taken of 2210 was immense and so welcome was the young company that they were invited on to the footplate to take photographs of the cab fittings, and have the technicalities of engine driving explained. To outward appearances the mileage record of engine No 2210 must have been abysmal; but as suggested earlier there may have been some clandestine assignments with which Doncaster and his friends were not familiar.

There were in all 20 engines of the 2210 class, of which the second ten were originally turned out with the domeless straightback boilers. Not all of them led such sedentary existence as No 2210. At one time five were stationed at Swindon, and they worked variously to Neath, via the Severn Tunnel and via Gloucester, to Weymouth, and one turn to London. As Reading was very much involved in the latter duty it comes into the present context in an amusing way. The 5.10pm standard gauge express from Paddington, non-stop to Reading in 45min, for the 36 miles, started out with 16 six-wheeled coaches. But at Slough five were slipped for the Windsor line. Only four miles further west, at Taplow, another three were slipped to be worked forward to Maidenhead and thence up the High Wycombe branch. Finally at Twyford, a further three coaches were slipped for Henley, leaving only five attached to the engine when the train arrived at Reading. In later years connoisseurs of railway working were always intrigued at the idea of the Cornish Riviera Express carrying three slip portions, to be detached at Westbury, Taunton and Exeter; but to detach three slip portions within a start-to stop run of 36 miles was *some* going. During his training at Swindon Works the famous engineer-author, E. L. Ahrons, occasionally rode on the footplate of the engine working this train, and he has described how it took 'the most frantic efforts on the part of a perspiring army of Paddington ticket collectors' to get the passengers into the right section of the train, but how they usually arrived at Reading with a fair number who wanted to be at Windsor, Marlow or Henley!

Doncaster and some of his friends from the north usually travelled by the Midland to Birmingham, there transferring from New Street to Snow Hill station to continue by Great Western. While waiting for the Birkenhead–Paddington express there was time for some photography, all the more welcome for the goings and comings of the Northern Division engines based and maintained at Wolverhampton. This division was under the command of the mighty George Armstrong, though the schoolboy enthusiasts were not to know then that it was because of his tremendous, and autocratic personality that Wolverhampton engines were painted in a style distinctive from that of Swindon, and included many technical differences, quite apart from outward signs like the shape of chimney caps, and the incidence of fireboxes raised above the level of the boiler. Doncaster and his friends travelled south by the crack Birkenhead–Paddington express, leaving Birmingham in the early afternoon and nicknamed the Northern Zulu. It stopped at Leamington and Oxford, and ran thence non-stop to Paddington. Their arrival at Reading was by slip coach, and because of the peculiar layout of the old station this posed an operating problem. To avoid the necessity of crossing over and threading a way through the platform road the coach was slipped at full speed from the train which continued on the main line, and pulled into the station by a chain horse.

The use of horses for shunting vehicles to be attached or detached from passenger trains did not apply only to unusual, far-off things on the Great Western Railway, because during the inter-war period, when the 5.15pm two-hour non-stop express from Bristol to Paddington slipped a coach at Swindon it was detached at full speed on the through line, and towed into the platform by a horse; still more archaic, though, was the practice at Bath employed even after I came to live in the City, from 1948 onwards. To certain up trains four-wheeled vacuum-fitted vehicles had to be attached at the rear. There was a short spur at the western end of the up platform, before its subsequent extension out on to the river bridge, where these vehicles would be parked and loaded, and a horse was stabled alongside. When the train arrived and its rearmost vehicle was clear of the points from the spur Dobbin would be coupled up, give a smart pull to the four-wheeler, and then step equally smartly out of the way; by this original method of fly-shunting the four-wheeler would ride gently ahead into contact with the rear of the standing train.

In 1894 a camera club was formed at the school Doncaster attended, and he and his three fellow railway enthusiasts promptly joined. Until then their activities had been entirely 'on the side' as it were, and their presence in and around the station, and at vantage points by the lineside had been regarded with an amused and benevolent tolerance by such authority as saw them. But as members of the school camera club they now had an official status, and with characteristic schoolboy audacity they determined to use

13

it. Across the tracks beyond the range of all their cameras were those engine sheds; the locomotives outside were enough to whet anyone's appetite, but who knew what treasures were ensconced *inside*? How the approach was made, and to whom I did not learn, but believe it or not permission was granted for those four boys to visit Reading engine sheds and to take photographs to their heart's content. In securing such a privilege, for such youthful enthusiasts I cannot help feeling that their application must have had some fairly strong support from the school authorities, although from what Doncaster himself told me their interests were not looked upon with any great favour by other boys and some of the masters. Unlike the preparatory school that I attended in Reading some 20 years later, participation in games was not compulsory, and for that quartet the engine sheds held far greater attractions than the cricket field.

At the time of the gauge conversion the Great Western had an incredible miscellany of standard gauge locomotives. The prospect of sudden removal from traffic of a considerable number of broad gauge engines in May 1892, had made it necessary to retain on the active list many old and otherwise obsolete types that any self-respecting administration would long ago have sent to the scrap yard. The standardisation that became such a dominant feature of Great Western locomotive practice in the new century would then have seemed as far off as the abolition of steam traction. The variety in styles, origins, and liveries bade fair to match that found on the North Eastern in the time of Edward Fletcher; nearly all of them moreover were very small. But I cannot think that the older and less spectacular specimens would have attracted the attention of young photographers struggling with very un-handy apparatus had they not all been so incredibly clean! The large brass dome cover of a little 0–4–2 tank propped up on end for repairs inside the shed was just as lovingly polished as that of a Dean 7ft 8in single passing through Reading non-stop at the head of the Cornishman. Following that first meeting Doncaster and I exchanged photographs many times, and I had the honour of using some of his results in my own articles. But what of the engines they saw and photographed at Reading?

Locomotive photography was then a matter of pure guess-work for the amateur. After all, such guidance as might be given as to exposure by the manufacturers of glass plates hardly extended to subjects in the dark recesses of engine sheds; and there, inevitably,

14

were to be found some of the choicest specimens. While not disclosing how many plates were ruined in the early 'hit or miss' stages, Doncaster certainly secured some excellent pictures later, none finer than one of an Armstrong 0–6–0 goods engine of 1873, underneath one of the smoke extracting ducts, but polished to the last rivet head, with the cab fittings glittering like the contents of a jeweller's shop. This particular engine was one of a class introduced by Joseph Armstrong and it retained all the Swindon characteristics in the shape of the copper capped chimney and dome towards the forward end of the boiler. There was also not the slightest outward sign of ownership either on engine or tender, save for an inconspicuous works plate on the framing just above the horn guides for the middle pair of coupled wheels. In the era of mixed gauges they were about the nearest the Great Western ever got to a standard engine class, but when some of them went to the Northern Division and big brother George got his hands on them they emerged from Wolverhampton Works painted in his own shade of green, with rolled top chimney caps, and his own very effective setting of the Stephenson link motion.

The variety in 2–4–0s alone to be seen around Reading was astonishing, and if one included those that might also be glimpsed at Oxford or Birmingham it was enough to put even the North Eastern in the shade. At that time, however, even before the coming of the Dean 7ft 8in singles, it was the 2–2–2 and not the 2–4–0 that was the premier standard gauge passenger type. The 2210 that was standing pilot at the western end of Reading station for so long was actually one of the most modern varieties of 2–4–0, which with 6ft 6in coupled wheels could probably have run well up to the maximum speeds required by the standard gauge trains of those days. The very similar, but smaller wheeled 481 class 2–4–0s were also occasionally to be seen and photographed at Reading. In Doncaster's day these were rebuilds of an older and smaller 2–4–0 class that had run the very slow passenger trains on the Berks & Hants line, and as such were no strangers at Reading; after rebuilding most of them were transferred to Bristol to work on the through West to North expresses via the Severn Tunnel, where their 6ft wheels were considered an advantage in surmounting the heavy gradients of that route.

Around 1890 the Great Western locomotive department seemed to be in two minds as to whether to finalise on inside or outside frames, and while the 2210 series and the smaller wheeled 481 class represented one school of thought, in 1889 Swindon turned out the very handsome 3206 class of 2–4–0 with 6ft coupled wheels and the double sandwich type of frame, in the style of the broad gauge 8ft singles. There were 20 of these engines, to be followed very soon after by an enlarged version of the 2210 with inside frames! The sandwich framed 3206 class did not appear to work to Reading at the time Doncaster was at school there, but I remember them very well myself in their later form, when they had domeless parallel boilers and high raised Belpaire fireboxes. To my boyish eyes they looked awkward mis-shapen things; but the point that remains with me is that they were used sometimes on expresses between Paddington and Reading. There was a train for the Weymouth line that used to come down from London hauled by one of them, and at Reading a 4–4–0 would take over.

Constructional policy about the time of the gauge conversion seemed to be the very opposite of the 'scrap and build' philosophy developed later, and some remarkable cases of rebuilding were enacted at Swindon in the 1890s. Perhaps the most extraordinary was that of the eight 2–2–2s of the 69 class built at Wolverhampton in 1872–75, which 20 years later were converted into 2–4–0s. On one of his journeys south, when the train drew up at Banbury, Doncaster spotted old No 69 on another train taking water. He leapt out of the train and got a picture that was indeed historic, because in a very short time the engine had been rebuilt. It goes perhaps almost without saying that the old 2–2–2 was still in beautiful external condition. The rebuild was remarkable in that a new section of sandwich frame was added at the rear end to accommodate the second pair of coupled wheels. The open splasher over the original single pair of driving wheels was closed in, while the new coupling rods were outside. More interesting still, the rebuilt engines were named after rivers, and were the first standard gauge engines other than single wheelers to be so distinguished. It was fortunate that there were so many rivers in the West Country with short names because nothing longer than five letters could be accommodated on the splasher between the spring hanger, which was above the frame. The eight engines became *Avon, Dart, Dee, Exe, Isis, Stour, Teign,* and *Wye.* The two largest rivers in Great Western territory, the Thames and Severn, were discarded, as too long for the nameplate space!

Doncaster and his friends saw many of the 2–2–2 singles going through Reading, including the unique 7ft 8in engine No 9, with outside Stephenson link motion; these engines never found their way into Reading sheds, and so escaped the camera barrage that would otherwise have awaited them. Instead, energies were concentrated on the variety of tank engines then to be seen. Looking at a range of photographs taken at that time it would seem quite incredible that so many different shapes, sizes, and styles could have been evolved, even granting that they came from two different works, which in their turn had inherited many from some smaller constituent companies. It would seem also that when the time came for them to be repaired one works or the other put on just those features or fittings that the erecting shop foreman had readily available. So it happened that engines originally of Wolverhampton origin could be seen with Swindon type boiler mountings and Swindon style of painting, for no matter how humdrum or menial the duties a Great Western engine must not be anything but immaculate.

But after 1892 the Great Western was moving into a new age. Financially the company had survived the upheaval of the final gauge conversion remarkably well, and the dividend on the ordinary shares which had stood at $6\frac{1}{4}$ per cent in 1891 had fallen no lower than $4\frac{3}{4}$ in 1893, and had rallied to 6 per cent again by 1896. The whole outlook of the company was buoyant, and I cannot leave the Reading of the 19th century without referring to the complete reconstruction of the station, which was begun in 1896 and finished in 1899. It was a tremendous task though curiously enough one that received little notice in the railway press of the day. When it is recalled that before the change the station was approached from the London direction on no more than two running lines, and that the complicated and inconvenient track layout was tucked in between the main block of station buildings and the engine shed, it meant that to provide six through running lines, four, instead of one, lengthy platform faces, lavish new facilities and bay platforms at both ends, nothing short of a completely clean sweep would be needed. When the broad gauge was abolished all that was done at first was to remove the outermost rail, the entire layout having been mixed gauge for some time previously, and the Brunel type bridge rails with longitudinal timbers remained.

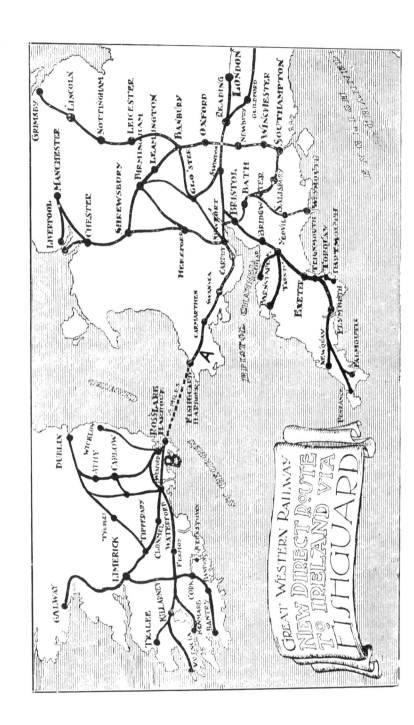

GREAT WESTERN RAILWAY
NEW DIRECT ROUTE TO IRELAND VIA FISHGUARD

2
Sir Felix Pole: Some Recollections

There was a time, long years ago, when personalities loomed large in the British railway world. In the years around the first world war timetable sheets displayed on station platforms bore the name 'Frank Potter, General Manager', and one did not have to turn through very many numbers of *The Railway Magazine* to find what he looked like. In that era, and for nearly 20 years subsequently 'The Railway Portrait Gallery' was a prominent feature in that journal. It was after the death of J. F. Gairns, for so long the Editor, and the merging of the editorial staff with that of *The Railway Gazette* that a degree of rationalisation in the coverage of railway news took place, and thence-forward personalia vanished from *The Railway Magazine*, more was the pity. In July 1919 Frank Potter died, at the early age of 63 years. He had been General Manager since 1912, and there is little doubt that the strain of the war years and of the very high responsibilities that he carried shortened his life. He was succeeded by Charles Aldington, who only a few months previously had been appointed to the new post of Assistant General Manager, having himself been Superintendent of the Line since 1910. In July 1919, the directors appointed as the new Assistant General Manager, Felix J. C. Pole, who had been Chief Clerk to the General Manager from 1913, and his portrait appeared in *The Railway Magazine*.

Before 1913 Pole's career, entirely in the service of the Great Western Railway, had been most varied. He joined the company when 14 years of age as a telegraph boy at Swindon in 1891, but on being appointed to the personal staff of the Chief Engineer, James Inglis in 1896, his enthusiasm for the railway led to him becoming Editor of the *Great Western Railway Magazine*, entirely as a spare time job done at home. But it was not long before this was adopted as an official staff publication, and Pole continued to be responsible for it until he was appointed Assistant General Manager of the company. In 1903 Inglis was appointed General Manager, continuing to hold his previous post of Chief Engineer for a short time, and in 1904 Pole also transferred to the General Manager's office. While there, in 1906, he contributed a notable article to *The Railway Magazine* on the new route to Ireland, via Fishguard and Rosslare. It was a meaty piece, showing his obvious flair for attractive descriptive writing, and a full appreciation of all the technical features in the very difficult constructional work in the new harbour and railway station. He did not fail to stress the potentialities of Fishguard as a future Transatlantic port.

Today however, the most intriguing feature of that finely illustrated 10-page article is the map, which is reproduced on page 18. With Pole it always seemed to be a case of 'GWR first, and the rest nowhere'! And if he was not the actual cartographer of that map we may be sure he was at the elbow of the man who drew it, in the way potential traffic from a goodly proportion of the South of England is shown funnelling into the South Wales main line at Newport. The extension by Great Central connections to Leicester and Nottingham is interesting, no less in their north easterly extension to Lincoln and Grimsby, while the continuation northward from Shrewsbury to Liverpool and Manchester via Chester, is amusing in its audacity, and in the complete absence of such a nodal point as Crewe from the map!

Aldington was in poor health, and in the summer of 1921 he retired from the general managership, whereupon Pole got the job, at the early age of 44. James Milne who was later to succeed him, was appointed Assistant General Manager, and it fell to him to carry on in the late autumn of 1923 when Pole was away in the Sudan, preparing a report on the Government Railways. Largely as a result of this work Pole was knighted, in 1924. By that time in its post war recovery the Great Western was veritably riding on the crest of a wave. It was largely due to him that, released from Government wartime control the company had restored full pre-war standards of speed on all its principal express routes for the winter service of 1921. He had indeed begun to take the reins even before Aldington felt compelled to retire, because of the latter's long absences from office due to ill-health. The problems facing Pole in 1921 were immense. The Railways Act of that year authorising the Grouping of the many individual lines into no more than four large companies had been passed by Parliament earlier that summer, and while the Great Western was likely to be least affected of any of the larger companies the process of amalgamation with such virile and hitherto prosperous concerns as the local railways in South Wales was likely to involve many serious problems. Furthermore he was worried about the basic top level organisation which had been virtually unchanged since the days of Brunel and Gooch.

In his younger days in the General Manager's office Pole had developed an almost fervent admiration for Sir James Inglis and his methods, and it would have been surprising if some whispers of the tremendous top-level row that raged between the General Manager and some senior officers had not come to the ears of one so relatively 'near to the throne' as Pole. From the earliest days senior officers like the Locomotive, Carriage and Wagon Superintendent, and the Chief Engineer had reported direct to the respective committees of the Board, and they had attended Board meetings in their own right. There is a story told that on one occasion when Inglis was Chief Engineer, and the then General Manager Sir Joseph Wilkinson had queried some matter that appertained to engineering, Inglis had told him bluntly to mind his own business! But there was more to it than that. Each of the major departments did its own accounting, on principles established quite unilaterally, and at times it was no end of a task to coordinate the overall company results, on which the dividend would have to be based. When he moved up to become General Manager Inglis quickly realised the anomaly of the system and sought to alter it by proposing a new organisation in which all the senior officers reported to the General Manager. Lord Churchill, who became Chairman in 1908, saw the force of this argument, and approved it. But there were some stormy meetings of the Board at which the chief officers likely to lose their autonomy by this scheme fought tooth and nail against it.

Inglis was very upset by the storm that had arisen. Although a majority of the Board approved it, and copies of the new organisational tree were signed by the Chairman for issue to each of the chief officers affected, they were never sent out, and Pole found them secreted away in the General Manager's safe when he took office in 1921. Much that had been hearsay and rumour to him ten to a dozen years earlier, when he was little more than a junior in the General Manager's office, now became clear; while recognising the cogency of the scheme Inglis had worked out, but refrained from putting into effect because of his own gentleness of nature, its two principal opponents among the senior staff were still in office, with one at least having reached a towering status in the railway world. It need hardly be added that one was G. J. Churchward; the second was W. W. Grierson, the Chief Engineer. Moreover, both seemed in excellent health, unaffected by the strains of the war years that had told so heavily on some of their contemporaries on other railways. Pole saw clearly enough that the Inglis scheme of reorganisation was unquestionably right, but an examination of the Board minutes of those stormy days of 1908–10 gave a clear enough indication of where the opposition lay, and in Churchward's case his attitude was not likely to have softened with the years! Nevertheless Pole felt there would be no harm in putting out what he hoped would be a tactful feeler, and suggested that there was really no need for him to go to the trouble of coming up to London for a short Board meeting. He got an instant rebuff: 'Look here, Pole, when my Chairman tells me to stop away, I'll stop away – not before!' And that was that.

That courteous approach, despite his instantly hostile reaction to it, evidently carried some weight with Churchward. Although he was then in his 65th year there were then no fixed ages at which senior officers were asked to retire, and indeed his successor continued until he was 70. But after the war the trade unions involved at Swindon and among the footplate men were beginning to exert their influence; when at one slightly difficult meeting he was told that the men expected to be *consulted* on future policy rather than just informed, he reluctantly saw the way the wind was blowing. This, together with the presence of that exceedingly dynamic young man of 44 in the 'driving seat' at Paddington persuaded him that it was time to retire. He was a countryman at heart, and had many hobbies, and so he went at the end of 1921. Pole saw to it that his successor was appointed under the terms of the Inglis plan, and with Grierson's retirement at the end of 1923 the transition in top level organisation was complete. As Pole himself put it when I was with him some years after his own retirement from business: 'I became the first General Manager of the Great Western Railway', and in the sense that the GM was the chief executive officer through whom all others reported this was certainly true.

My first contact with him came in unexpected circumstances. In the summer of 1924 I graduated at London University, and

Imperial College, with an honours degree in engineering, but as I was then no more than 19 my father thought that the chances of my getting a job at once were slender. He therefore arranged for me to take a post-graduate course and meanwhile the opportunities for beginning a career could be explored in more leisure than during the tremendous rush and tear leading up to the degree examination. My father was a branch manager in Barclays Bank, and at one stage of our explorations, towards the end of 1924, he wrote to what would now be called the personnel department of the bank to try and obtain an introduction to the railway service. The result was startling, because the high bank official concerned happened to be a friend of Sir Felix Pole! A week or so passed, and then with a covering letter from the bank headquarters in London my father received a handwritten note: 'F. J. C. Pole will see this young man on . . .' I shall never forget the high hopes with which I went to Paddington on the appointed day, nor of the disappointment I felt immediately afterwards, for it was partly a sense of bewilderment, and not really knowing what I expected from that interview. Many times since however I have pondered upon the wisdom of the advice and help he gave me.

At the time I was a little shocked at the brusque way in which he pushed aside details of my academic training, and the surprise he felt that so far no steps had been taken towards any practical training. 'Without that' he emphasised 'We don't get any forrader'. At this stage he called James Milne, then Assistant General Manager, into the room, and explained to him that I had got an engineering degree, but so far no workshop experience. Now Milne was a BSc himself, and had been trained as a locomotive engineer at Swindon, though his subsequent experience had been mainly on the traffic side, which I had noted from the biographical notes published in *The Railway Magazine* at the time of his appointment as assistant to Pole. It was explained to me that the GWR was then fully staffed with pupils in all their engineering departments; what else could they do for me. I said that I believed they took university graduates in the traffic departments, but Pole himself pulled me up short to say, 'not engineering ones', and proceeded to paint a depressing picture of the humdrum, purely clerical tasks to which trainees on the traffic side were subjected. 'You wouldn't like that', he added. Then, brisk as always, he promised to give me letters of introduction to various engineering firms from which they had purchased material, wished me the best of luck, and I was out!

How, through his introduction, I obtained a berth with the Westinghouse Brake & Saxby Signal Company, as it was then, as a graduate-trainee is another story, but I shall always remember the quite charming personal letter he wrote to me afterwards wishing me every success. I watched Great Western affairs, as an outside enthusiast, through the exciting days of the 1925 and 1926 locomotive interchange trials, the building of the Kings, and the visit of engine No 6000 to the USA, though it was only in more recent times that I came to realise the tremendous power behind the scenes that Sir Felix Pole was in exhorting his senior engineering executives to achievements that put the GWR so prominently in the very forefront of British locomotive practice. I sometimes wonder how its history might have run had he remained in the chair at Paddington during the 1930s when the Great Western thunder was so effectively stolen, first by one and then by the other of the north-going lines. I am sure the boot would have been put behind Collett as vigorously as it was over the building of the Kings. But in July 1929 Sir Felix resigned from the GWR to take up the office of Chairman of Associated Electrical Industries. He was still only 52 years of age, and at the very peak of his railway achievements; he was to guide AEI through 18 of the most dramatic years in the history of British industry.

The story now moves to the year 1946, when the bookselling and publishing firm of W. Heffer & Sons, of Cambridge approached me for a book about the Great Western Railway. At the time my literary work had only just begun to develop from articles in the railway and technical press to full-length books, and I was thrilled beyond measure. Apparently, after the war Heffers had recruited on their staff a young man who was a railway enthusiast, and he had persuaded the management to undertake publication of some railway books. The late Cecil J. Allen was invited to contribute a book on locomotive practice and performance, while in view of the impending dissolution of the existing railway management structure, by nationalisation, their plans included four books, one each about the main line companies of the Grouping Era. I understood that Cecil J. Allen was to do that on the London & North Eastern Railway, and other authors were suggested for the Southern and the LMS. But in the event mine, on the GWR was the only one that ever got off the ground, and then only after a very long delay on the publishers' part. But the book was commissioned in the summer of 1946, and I began work at once. It was to be an appreciation of the railway as a going concern: not a definitive history, nor a study of management policy or techniques, but containing enough of a 'behind the scenes' atmosphere as to attract those enthusiasts who looked for a little more than mere lineside, and platform-end observation. Sir James Milne, the last, and according to Pole only the second General Manager of the GWR, gave the project his blessing, and with the enthusiastic help of Major J. Dewar, the Publicity Officer, I set out on a memorable round of exploration.

It was nevertheless not an ideal time to do the field work for such a project. I had hardly started when the fearful winter of 1946–7 was upon us. In anticipation of the re-establishment of the Westinghouse London office at Kings Cross from its wartime quarters at Chippenham, my family, like that of many others had returned to our pre-war home, and I was travelling between Chippenham and Paddington most week-ends and in very truth I saw the GWR in adversity. As opportunity presented itself appointments were made for me to talk to senior officers, and it was remarkable how frequently reminiscences of Sir Felix Pole's time as General Manager came up, even from some who could not have been more than juniors in his time. Except when he was abroad on AEI business he travelled daily between Paddington and Reading, west of which latter town he lived in a beautiful home, Calcot Grange, lying just north of the Bath Road. It was a source of much pleasure to him when one of the 6800 class of mixed traffic 4–6–0s, built in 1936 in replacement of some of the 4300 class of 2–6–0s, No 6833 was named *Calcot Grange*. Those who spoke of him referred to his remarkable memory for people, and faces, even after his sight began to fail. He had occasion to meet Major Dewar just at the end of the war, and said: 'Ah, Dewar; how's your rheumatism?' The poor man was nearly crippled with it.

Pole retired from the Chairmanship of AEI in the early autumn of 1945, due to increasingly severe eye trouble; but the great company that he had served with such energy and success for 16 years would not let him go, and he remained as Deputy Chairman. I would have had no occasion to seek an interview with Sir Felix in connection with the book on which I commenced to work in 1946, and knowing of his affliction I felt it would have been inopportune to make any such approach. Because of the difficulties of the time the book was a long time in drafting and I did not send the script to Heffers until early in 1948, by which time the Great Western

Railway had ceased to exist. Sir James Milne had been offered the Chairmanship of the nationalised Railway Executive, and turned it down, and everyone in the newly designated Western Region was in the dumps. For a space of very nearly two years also the fate of my book hung in the balance. As a newcomer to the firm I could not ask too many questions, but I gathered that its entry in the world of railway publishing had not met with the success anticipated.

My own book was not published until 1951, and I learned that a copy was sent to Sir Felix Pole, who by that time was completely blind. It was evident that he still took the keenest interest in matters concerning his old railway, and had the book read to him from cover to cover. Not knowing anything of this it was a great surprise one day to receive a letter which he had dictated, but signed personally in much the same hand that I remembered so well from my contact with him 27 years earlier. He had evidently been through it very carefully, but his principal comment took me rather aback. He thought it rather extraordinary that in a book about the Great Western Railway there was only a passing reference, in the preface, to the General Manager, and no mention at all of the Board of Directors. I wrote back explaining that my remit, from the publisher had been to write an 'appreciation' of the railway, as seen by an outsider, and that reference to high policy and such like were really beyond my scope. I heard no more at the time, but a wonderful surprise was in store for me in the following years.

About the time the Heffer book was published I was getting involved with other literary work concerning the Great Western, and this time far more with personalities than previously. My friends at Paddington said that I ought to see Sir Felix, and when I demurred on account of his blindness, they reassured me, saying that he'd love it. And so it turned out. At first that meeting was not too easy to arrange. I was then Chief Draughtsman of the Westinghouse Brake & Signal Company, my duties embracing not only brakes and signals, but rectifiers, steam heating and colliery work, and I was often out at week-ends in addition to being pretty well tied up all the week. A Saturday seemed the only possible time, but I was intrigued when Sir Felix indicated to my friends at Paddington that this would suit him admirably, and would I care to meet him at Swindon? How things were eventually contrived that I should meet him there on a day when I had an important evening engagement there on the very same day I cannot now recall; but I can say this, that when I walked out of the station to find him sitting in a beautiful black chauffeur driven limousine I had still no idea of what he had in store.

With him was one of his grandsons, whom he introduced as 'Fe-fi-fo-fum'! I learned afterwards that he also was a Felix Pole. With surprising agility for one so afflicted he got out of the car, and on the arm of his very young grandson entered the station, was piloted up the stairs on to the down platform, and asked to be guided to the famous dining rooms. He was intensely proud of the association he had forged between the Great Western and the Baltimore & Ohio Railroad at the time of the latter company's centenary in 1927. It was intended to celebrate the centenary in a very big way, and some years beforehand its President, Daniel Willard, commissioned a noted American railway enthusiast, Ed Hungerford by name, to collect data and relics and to formulate proposals. In 1925 he came to England to see how the railway centenary was celebrated, and in the course of his stay here he met Sir Felix Pole. During various discussions he confided to him that Daniel Willard would very much like to have an English locomotive in the great pageant he was organising. Sir Felix was delighted, and to him of course an 'English' locomotive could not mean anything but a Great Western! By the summer of 1925 the Castle class 4–6–0s had taken the British railway world by storm. The published results of the dynamometer car trials with *Caldicot Castle* between Swindon and Plymouth in 1924 had shaken the locomotive fraternity of the northern lines to their foundations, while the dashing exploits of the same engine, and of *Pendennis Castle* in the interchange trials with the LNER early in 1925 had greatly impressed popular opinion. To send a Castle to the USA in 1927 was therefore merely to blaze their reputation internationally and Pole was delighted to agree.

A large volume of water was to flow beneath Great Western bridges between the 1925 meeting between Sir Felix and Ed Hungerford, and the actual arrival of a Swindon engine in the USA in 1927; but the events of those two years show so clearly his drive, his grip on affairs and his strength of personality, no less than his intense enthusiasm for anything Great Western – as to make necessary an extended reference to those events, as a prelude to studying that *pièce de résistance* in the dining room at Swindon to which his grandson was to be bidden to lead us.

The exciting saga began in August 1926, when the Southern Railway in producing the *Lord Nelson* threw an almighty spanner into the works. The Great Western no longer had the most powerful express locomotive in Great Britain! The new Southern 4–6–0 had a nominal tractive effort of 33,510 lb against the 31,625 lb of the Castle and the publicity people at Waterloo were not backward in telling the world all about it! Sir Felix Pole was shocked and immediately summoned Collett, and told him he must do something about it. Now the Chief Mechanical Engineer, unlike his great predecessor, was not the man to worry overmuch about publicity. He had been rather disturbed over the acrimonious aftermath of the 1925 locomotive interchange trials with the LNER and was apparently quite content with the Castle as his first-line express passenger type. He was primarily a workshop man, always intent upon improving production methods and reducing costs. When Pole asked for more powerful engines he simply replied that he had built up to the limit the Chief Engineer would permit, namely a maximum axle load of $19\frac{1}{2}$ tons. This figure touched a chord in Pole's remarkable memory, and his previous association with Sir James Inglis, both in the Engineer's and in the General Manager's department; while Collett was still there he summoned the Chief Engineer, J. C. Lloyd, who revealed that ever since the days of Inglis all new bridges had been built to take a static axle-load of 22 tons, and as older ones were repaired they too had been strengthened to the same standard. The Locomotive Department had been kept in the dark. When Lloyd also said that only *four* bridges remained to be strengthened to make the entire Paddington–Plymouth route capable of taking a 22-ton axle load he was told to press on with it as a matter of urgency.

Collett was instructed to proceed at once with the design of a new express passenger locomotive of maximum power, and have it ready for the summer traffic of 1927. Lloyd was asked if he could accept $22\frac{1}{2}$ tons as the maximum axle-load, and when he agreed the work at Swindon began. After Pole resolved this point at issue between the civil and the mechanical engineering departments, and set them both going on a major new project, an unexpected opportunity came to boost still further the merits of Great Western locomotive practice. He was a great friend of Sir Guy Granet, Chairman of the LMS; and in that summer of 1926 he learned of Sir Guy's increasing anxiety over the continuing friction and divergence in views between the operating and the mechanical engineering departments on his railway. Earlier Sir Henry Fowler had been authorised to build some huge four-cylinder compound Pacific engines in the French style, but the operating department were so incensed that by some intense counter-lobbying they got the project halted, though not before the frames for the two new engines had been cut. Though there is no factual evidence to support this next point it would not have been in the least surprising if Pole, hearing of the dilemma in which Sir Guy Granet found himself, had not said: 'Try one of ours'. And this, of course, is what the LMS actually did, and engine No 5000 *Launceston Castle*, did some experimental running between Euston and Carlisle in November 1926.

Meanwhile Pole's thoughts had turned once again to the forthcoming centenary of the Baltimore & Ohio Railroad, and by more vigorous prodding of Collett having secured that the new super-express passenger 4–6–0s would have a nominal tractive effort slightly over 40,000 lb he decided that the Great Western exhibit at the B & O centenary celebrations should not be a Castle but one of the new engines. There was no question of whether it could be done in time; it was an order! The late Kenneth J. Cook was then Assistant Locomotive Works Manager, and he told me of the dramatic way in which the news was received at Swindon in December 1926. By that time very little in the way of drawings had been received in the works, in fact no more than outline diagrams. One day he was called to the office of his chief, R. A. G. Hannington; Stanier, then Principal Assistant to the CME was there, and he was asked how things were progressing with the new engines. From the information already received he told them that he was expecting to have the first engine completed by about the end of October 1927, at which point Stanier cut him short, saying: 'Young man, she's got to be in the USA by August!' And so the race was on.

As for the diverse factors that between them led to the design and construction of the King class locomotives, in 1927, A. W. J. Dymond, on whose drawing board the design of the special bogie took shape, and Hawksworth himself who as Chief Draughtsman was responsible for the detailed design of the locomotive can add some detail, particularly about the bogie. From these accounts the very authenticity of which is guaranteed by the personalities from whom they originated, one turns with interest, and not a little curiosity, to the reference to the new engines in the Annual Report of the Chief Mechanical Engineer for the Year 1926, and dated December of that year. It reads:

The construction of 20 engines of the Castle type has had to be deferred owing to difficulties arising out of the coal strike, and as recent investigations of the Bridge Stress Committee, under the Department of Scientific and Industrial Research, have now clearly established that our four-cylinder balanced type of engine has a much less detrimental effect on bridges than that of any other type, it is now proposed to build these 20 engines to a heavier and more powerful design. It is hoped that some of the principal main lines routes of the Railway on which for some years the new bridges have been built stronger, will be ready for use of the heavier engines at an early date. This will enable the heavy summer traffic to be handled more satisfactorily and with greater economy.

This report was no doubt prepared for the Board, and perhaps for some of the largest and most influential shareholders; while not questioning its accuracy in most respects, it does not, somewhat naturally, reflect the true situation of a rather troubled period between the Chief Mechanical Engineer and the top management of the railway. The balancing of the four-cylinder Star class 4–6–0 locomotives as first revealed by the Bridge Stress Committee, for example, was anything but satisfactory. Until that time it was the practice at Swindon, with the four-cylinder engines, to balance a proportion of the reciprocating parts separately for the inside and outside cylinders, in the leading and middle pairs of coupled wheels respectively. Although the balance applied to the leading coupled axle was opposed to that of the middle one, and the total engine hammerblow was relatively small, the hammerblow from each of the individual axles actually exceeded that of the two-cylinder Saints! It was only when this situation was discovered in the course of the Bridge Stress Committee's report that the method of balancing was revised to the very satisfactory arrangement subsequently adopted also on the Castles and which paved the way for the Kings.

At the same time it was not quite correct to say that the Great Western 'four-cylinder balanced type of engine' had a much less detrimental effect on bridges than *any* other type. Maybe this was correct so far as the locomotives examined by the Bridge Stress Committee were concerned. But the ex-LNWR four-cylinder 4–6–0s of the Claughton class, with cranks equally spaced, and all four cylinders driving on to one axle had no hammerblow at all, and for that reason no trial runs were made with them at the time of the Bridge Stress Committee's work.

The cleverly faked-up 'photograph' of the 'New Heavy Powerful Engine' included in the Chief Mechanical Engineer's Report for 1926 is extremely interesting as giving documentary evidence of an important intermediate stage in the evolution of the King design. The faked photograph clearly reveals the original intention to use the standard 6ft 8½in driving wheels, and a standard Churchward bogie, as on the Castle class, the latter with inside frames throughout. The tractive effort, in the Report, was specified as 39,000 lb, which would result from the use of 16¼in by 28in, cylinders, and an increase in boiler pressure to 250 lb/sq in. The actual value would have been 39,155 lb, but 39,000 was near enough to quote on an illustration of so preliminary a nature.

It was at that stage that Sir Felix Pole intervened, and urged Collett to boost up the tractive effort to surpass the 40,000 lb mark. This was easily done, on paper, by reducing the diameter of the coupled wheels to 6ft 6in, but the complications and the expense were not confined to making new patterns and tooling for a size of coupled wheel that was new in modern Great Western practice. Hawksworth, as a true disciple of Churchward, determined that the centre line of the cylinders must be horizontal and therefore they would have to be lowered 1¼in from the Castle position, and being of slightly larger diameter in addition there arose problems of clearance beneath the inside cylinders. The situation was complicated because at about this period there had been a number of failures with the Churchward bar framed bogie, through rivets breaking, and it was felt that a plate-framed job would be better.

A. W. J. Dymond was given the job of designing the new bogie, and he soon found that with the reduced clearance beneath the cylinders, because of their lowered position, that although the diameter of the bogie wheels was to be reduced from 3ft 2in to 3ft, it was going to be extremely difficult to work in inside plate frames of adequate depth, particularly in view of the apparent need to design a stronger bogie to obviate the kind of failures that they had lately been experiencing. So, recalling the outside-framed bogies that had been standard on the Dean inside-cylinder 4–2–2 and 4–4–0 engines he put forward the idea of a hybrid bogie, with outside frames for the leading wheels, and inside frames for the after pair. This design was adopted, and in consequence the actual front end of the King class locomotives looked rather different from that faked up photograph in the report of December 1926.

How magnificent an impression *King George V* created in the

USA is a matter of history; Daniel Willard of the B&O wrote in most glowing terms to Sir Felix Pole soon afterwards. The engine had been hailed as 'a distinguished envoy' even before it arrived in the USA; its reputation soared to a positive crescendo of acclaim before it returned to England carrying the famous presentation bell on the buffer beam. It is said that imitation is the sincerest form of flattery and barely six months after the return of the locomotive Sir Felix Pole received a letter from C. W. Galloway, Vice President of the B&O reading thus:

> It might interest you to know that we have just finished a locomotive with water-tube back and eliminating entirely stay-bolts. This engine was designed by Col George H. Emerson, our Chief of Motive Power and Equipment, and was built at our Mt Clare shops, Baltimore. I am enclosing you a photograph of it. You will note we have copied the front end from the *King George V*, and endeavoured to copy the stack, but do not believe we got that quite right in the shape of the copper top. I might trespass upon you to impose the requests, if you have a plan of this stack, to send me one that we might copy it correctly.
>
> You will also note that we have endeavoured to eliminate all the trimmings usually found on the exterior of an American locomotive, and with the exception of the two air tanks for the automatic brakes we have concealed everything. The air pump is between the frame opposite the centre of the two back drivers.

And so I come back to Swindon on that early spring day in 1952, when young Felix Pole led his blind grandfather and me to the far end of that famous dining room to see the photograph that Vice-President Galloway sent over from Baltimore in 1928, of the new Pacific, the *President Cleveland*. The photograph was reproduced in *The Railway Magazine* for November 1928 under the caption 'An Anglicised American Locomotive'. Sir Felix then said: 'There you are Fe-fi-fo-fum; read what it says underneath the picture', and in a delightfully childish treble voice his grandson told us how that picture came to be in Swindon.

Next Sir Felix asked to be guided to the telegraph office which was then a single storey outbuilding on the London end of the down main line platform. I recalled that this was the very place where he had begun his railway career, in 1891, as a lad of 14; but I was not prepared for what happened when we walked inside. Speaking aside to the man in charge I told him who his very distinguished visitor was, meanwhile Sir Felix had asked to be guided to one of the telegraph instruments. He then proceeded to tap out, in morse code, all the letters of the alphabet at lightning speed. Then he turned round smiling and said: 'Good, I can still do it'. For a moment he spoke with pride in the place where his own railway career had begun, and then he said: 'Where's Mr Nock; we must go now, they'll be waiting for us at Marlborough'. It was a Saturday and another of his grandsons, E. S. Watts, then 16, was at Marlborough College, and he and another railway enthusiast friend were waiting to be taken out to lunch. It was a delightful party, at the Aylesford Arms, after which we all went back to the school to see the college's model railway in action. Sir Felix was very kindly taking me back to Swindon, where another engagement awaited me. But we took a roundabout route, so that he could show me the beautiful little village of Ramsbury, which had some boyhood associations for him, call briefly on some old friends, and thence over the Downs to an entrancing view of the Vale of the White Horse, before we dipped steeply down towards Swindon. That night I thought long about his great career, and felt honoured at the friendship extended to me.

3

On Slip Coaches, Brakes, and Bearings

The philosophy of the slip coach was a very old one on the railways of Britain, but although the Great Western was for most of its life the largest, and certainly the longest surviving exponent of the art it does not appear to have been the originator. That distinction is thought to rest with the London, Brighton & South Coast Railway, as early in railway history as February 1858. In that year the practice began of slipping a coach for Lewes and Eastbourne from one of the Brighton expresses at Haywards Heath; nevertheless the broad gauge Great Western was not long in following and slip coach services were introduced at Slough and Reading in December of that same year. At that early date there were no such things as continuous brakes, and the operation was a good deal more free and easy than it became in later years. The way in which some of these slip coach operations were conducted would be enough to make a modern railwayman's hair stand on end, though accidents appear to have been relatively few, and none serious.

Once the idea had caught on, the extent to which it was carried was remarkable, not only on the Great Western but on some other large English railways, notably the Great Northern, Great Eastern, and the Midland. Before the days of continuous brakes things were easier, if not as safe; on some other lines indeed the usage became greater in later years, and reached its maximum in the years just before the first world war. Continuous brakes or not it was a curiously unbalanced operation, both from the viewpoint of rolling stock working and passenger convenience. The Cornish Riviera Express when at the pinnacle of its fame was a strange example. During the winter months it left Paddington with a minimum load of 14 coaches, and of those no fewer than seven were contained in slip portions, to be detached successively at Westbury, Taunton and Exeter. Each of these portions had to have separate guards, each very experienced and responsible men, who had to carry out the specialised operation of slipping by the technique to be referred to later. I have sometimes wondered if the Great Western was ever tempted to detach the Kingsbridge through carriage by a slip at Brent, instead of including it in the Exeter portion, and working it forward by the semi-fast train that originated at Exeter, and followed soon after the passage of the Limited. But that would have involved yet another guard, as well as increasing the load for the engine over the severe gradients between Newton Abbot and Brent.

I have never thought to enquire how those specially equipped slip coaches, and their guards got back to Paddington, ready for the next day's run, for the slip operation could not be performed in reverse! During the winter season the up Cornish Riviera Express rarely had more than eight coaches on when it arrived in Paddington. Until I knew the line better I had always been mystified by a remark in one of Cecil J. Allen's articles in *The Railway Magazine*, when he prefaced an account of running on the West of England main line thus: 'The curious point about the runs now to be described is that nearly all the friends to whom I am indebted for their details seem to have found the far West so entrancing that they never returned; in my file there are eleven runs in the down direction via Westbury, as compared with a modest three returning to town!' The explanation, as I myself discovered, was simple enough; the loads on the up expresses were so much less as to make the demands on locomotive power slight, by comparison. There were some trains that were heavier than the Torbay Limited as it was then styled, and the Riviera itself, but those who took details of train running did not often seem to travel by them.

The Great Western reached its zenith of slip coach operation in 1908, when no fewer than 79 were detached daily. Moreover the activity was so widely spread over the system that it took place at 43 different locations. In the 19th century, as the practice began to get into its stride, there were some cases that would strike us as being amusing, almost to the extent of hazardous. In the late 1860s there was a broad gauge train from Windsor to the Metropolitan line, which of course had to stop at Bishops Road to change engines; but believe it or not this train had a slip coach for Paddington main station! This apparently was detached just after the train passed Royal Oak, and it coasted along with an increasing distance behind the last coach of the main train, giving a very alert signalman just time to move the points and divert the slip coach into the main station. It was suggested that the only advantage from this extraordinary manoeuvre was to bring certain wealthy patrons immediately abreast of the cab rank, or perhaps senior officers of the GWR nearer to their headquarters offices!

The practice of slipping coaches in the near approaches to London did not rest at Royal Oak. In 1860 the Great Western, having secured a one-third share in the ownership of the West London Extension Railway, and thus extended its tentacles as far as Clapham Junction, saw, in the audacious westward advance of the London, Chatham & Dover Railway, and its proposal to build a West End terminus in Pimlico, an opportunity to extend its activities still further, and to the delight of the impecunious Chatham Company agreed to take a half-lease of the new station it was building adjacent to the well-established terminus of the London, Brighton & South Coast Railway. A share was taken in the cost of making the new bridge over the Thames wide enough to take the broad gauge, and the Chatham company agreed to lay the extra rails to make the tracks in the approach to the new terminus mixed gauge. The LCDR opened its station at Victoria in 1862, and in the following year the Great Western inaugurated a local train service into it from Southall. But then some genius at Paddington conceived the idea of providing a through express service from Bristol to Victoria! A coach from the morning up fast train was slipped abreast of where the present Old Oak Common carriage depot now is, and it was then taken via the West London and West London Extension lines and Latchmere junctions, round to Stewarts Lane and so to the Chatham main line. It involved nearly seven miles of the most curved and junction-infested railway around London; even if there were no signal checks I would think they would have done well to cover it in 20 minutes. It is not surprising that this slip coach service lasted less than a year, because if any passenger from the West Country wanted to get to the neighbourhood of Victoria he would have got there much quicker by continuing to Paddington and taking a fast-stepping hansom cab.

But the Great Western continued to have many curiosities in the way of slip coach workings. There was a southbound express from Birmingham that slipped coaches at two stations only four miles apart, the first at Hatton and the second at Warwick. The first provided a service to Stratford-on-Avon, before the construction of the North Warwickshire Line, but why Warwick should also have

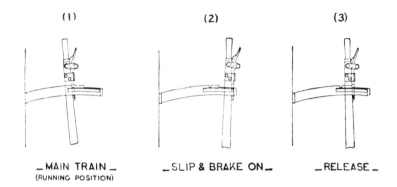

(1) _MAIN TRAIN_
(RUNNING POSITION)

(2) _SLIP & BRAKE ON_

(3) _RELEASE_

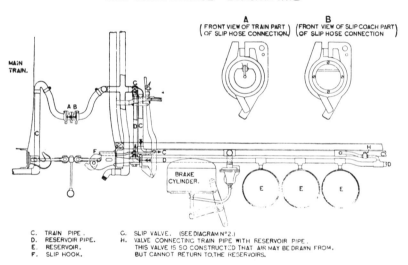

SLIP COACH WORKING   _DIAGRAM Nº1_

A
(FRONT VIEW OF TRAIN PART / OF SLIP HOSE CONNECTION)

B
(FRONT VIEW OF SLIP COACH PART / OF SLIP HOSE CONNECTION)

MAIN TRAIN.

BRAKE CYLINDER.

C. TRAIN PIPE.
D. RESERVOIR PIPE.
E. RESERVOIR.
F. SLIP HOOK.

G. SLIP VALVE. (SEE DIAGRAM Nº2.)
H. VALVE CONNECTING TRAIN PIPE WITH RESERVOIR PIPE.
    THIS VALVE IS SO CONSTRUCTED THAT AIR MAY BE DRAWN FROM.
    BUT CANNOT RETURN TO,THE RESERVOIRS.

Slip coach equipment. (*From the GWR General Appendix*)

been favoured when the main train would be stopping at
Leamington only two miles further on is indeed a puzzle to us
today, when many towns larger than Warwick are bereft of train
services altogether. In referring to odd services, long discontinued,
there cannot have been a more extraordinary case than one that
developed in the heat of the competition for London–Manchester
traffic between the Great Northern and the London & North

Western. By the 1880s the Great Northern had become badly infected by the slip-coach bug, and for a short time it was actually operating more than the Great Western; but why its crack 5.30pm from Kings Cross to Manchester, operated jointly with the Manchester, Sheffield & Lincolnshire Railway, should have been chosen to carry *four* slip portions is inexplicable. The first was detached at Huntingdon, and the second at Peterborough; meanwhile the main train went on non-stop to Grantham. There, while engines were being changed, a third slip portion was *attached* in rear, to be conveyed no more than $14\frac{1}{2}$ miles, and slipped at Newark. Finally, while the train was stopping at Retford, a fourth slip coach was attached, for a run of less than eight miles, to Worksop! Whether facilities were offered during the stops at Grantham and Retford for passengers who had travelled in the main train from London to nip smartly down the platform and join one or the other of the slip coaches is not related.

To return to the Great Western, the proliferation of slip coach services at Reading became a point of grievance with the inhabitants. While increasingly good facilities were provided for visitors arriving at their town there were no corresponding ways of getting out of it! But the traffic boffins at Paddington needed no little persuasion to insert additional stops into express train schedules. The tendency was to take them out. The train that Charles Doncaster and his school friends joined at Birmingham was a case in point. As mentioned in Chapter 1 of this book, in his travelling days it stopped at Oxford, but by the turn of the century it had a non-stop run from Leamington to Paddington, with slip portions detached at both Oxford and Reading. After the reconstruction of the latter station up expresses turned off the through line into the up main platform line so requiring a slack to about 30mph and a run I clocked in detail on the 5.15pm from Bristol to Paddington in 1936 showed what was involved in time, and by inference, in coal consumption. We had engine No 5048 then named *Cranbrook Castle*, but afterwards *Earl of Devon*, and were running at 75mph through Tilehurst. We slowed to 27mph through Reading and had recovered to 70mph by Twyford. With an unchecked run through Reading we could have done the distance between those two stations in about $2\frac{1}{2}$ minutes less; but figures subsequently published indicated that such a slowing, and the regaining of full speed afterwards used at least an extra hundredweight of coal.

A slip coach service at Reading that was revived after the second world war was that on the 8.30am from Plymouth to Paddington, a train that in GWR service was known from time immemorial as The Dutchman. This was a slip working that needed close and expert control between the driver and the slip guard, because in coming off the Berks & Hants line at Reading there was a severe speed restriction, first at Oxford Road Junction, just by Reading West station; it was continued round the curve, and over the trailing junctions on to the main line, but complicated in the case of the Dutchman by the need to maintain low speed while turning into and running through the up main platform line, where the slip coach came to rest. In any slip coach operation it was essential for the brakes to be fully released, and the reservoirs on the slip coach exhausted to the maximum degree of vacuum operated in the brake system so as to have what was sometimes called 'plenty of vacuum'. Thus in a case like that of the up Dutchman at Reading the brake application to reduce speed to the required figure had to be made well before reaching the station, so that the brakes could be released, and the system fully exhausted in time for the slip operation. The train would then be rolling freely, with perhaps a little steam on the locomotive, at around 30mph.

Great Western semaphore signalling in the 20th Century was characterised by very clear and well displayed groupings of the arms in junction layouts, and the home signal location at the exit from the Berks & Hants at Reading was exceptionally good. The elevated brackets structure carried four arms reading into the relief line part of the station (two arms), the up main line, and into the bay terminal platforms on the down side. These were followed when the main line itself was joined by others showing further bifurcations. But so far as slip coach working was concerned, although the semaphore for the up main might be lowered it did not necessarily mean that the line was clear right through the station and out on the London end. The signals were out of sight from the Berks & Hants line, but if a further check, or even a stop was involved it would not be possible to slip. To indicate to the driver and the slip guard whether there would be a clear run through the station additional distant arms were installed on the bracket post carrying the home signals at the end of the Berks & Hants line.

There was an amusing aside to this working at the time of the locomotive interchange trials organised by British Railways in 1948, soon after nationalisation. The up Dutchman was one of the trains included in the tests set to the visiting express passenger engines, and the strangers had to familiarise themselves with the brake working before slipping, and especially in the particular conditions of the Reading junctions. The Southern men were particularly intrigued, and their inimitable chief running inspector, the late Danny Knight, told me a good story. On the first up journey from Plymouth, with Merchant Navy class 4–6–2 No 35019 *French Line*, they successfully managed the slip operation, and duly arrived at Paddington. Now Danny was nothing if not a leg-puller. He was out on the platform chatting to the Western men when out of the corner of his eye he caught sight of one of the diesel railcar parcels vans running in. Clutching the arm of his Western *confrère*, he exclaimed: 'Blimey, we must have been going at Reading; here's our slip coach just arrived'.

In the 1920s both the 4.15 and 6.30pm expresses from Paddington to Plymouth (via Bristol) slipped a coach at Chippenham, in which I travelled on occasions. There were none of the complications of slipping at Reading on the up main platform line, because at Chippenham they were detached at full speed. Immediately after the arrival of the slip coach a steam rail motor coach, which had been standing in the bay platform, backed on, and the slip was conveyed forward to Bath and Bristol. Passengers from London could of course continue, and enjoyed an excellent through service from Paddington to Corsham, Box and Bathampton, though, of course, nothing approaching such a facility was available in the opposite direction. In later years, because, it was rumoured, of strong representations from the management of Westinghouse, the Chippenham slip coaches were discontinued, and a stop inserted. When the slip coaches were being worked senior executives of the firm, having spent a day in London, were not able to dine on the way home. The Great Western never adopted the London & North Western practice of having corridor slip coaches. In the case of Chippenham perhaps it was just as well, in case some of my former colleagues, dining possibly a little too well, might still have been in the restaurant car when the slip was detached!

My previous reference to the need for having plenty of vacuum on the slip portion, was vividly shown when one morning I travelled in the slip portion detached at Bath from the post-1945 9.5am from Paddington to Bristol. Until the high-speed Bristolian was put on in 1935 the morning service was really rather dreadful. Had it not been for the slip coach carried on the 8.55am South Wales express, and detached at Stoke Gifford (due in Temple Meads at 11.19am) there was no alternative to the purgatorial 9.15am from Paddington. But after the war a new express was put on, which ran non-stop from Reading to Bristol, slipping a section at Bath. This was particularly useful to Admiralty personnel, and the slip portion rarely consisted of less than three coaches. Although the act of slipping was carried out after speed had been reduced for the regulation slack through Bath it was not such a tricky job as that of the up Dutchman, at Reading. I had a number of good runs on this train, several on the footplate. It was allowed 76 minutes for the 70.9 miles from Reading to Bath, and on one of these when I was on *Nunney Castle* we slipped no fewer than four coaches. It was always a matter of importance on the engine to be sure the slip portion was safely away. Then one morning, when I was travelling to Bath, and we had enjoyed a good run down from London, we had passed through Sidney Gardens at about 30mph and the short tunnel, but immediately afterwards the brakes went on with a rush and the coach stopped in little more than its own length. I had just time to look out of the window and see the main part of the train disappearing cheerfully through Bath station. And there we were – well and truly stuck! By some mischance, when the slip portion was detached from the main train the valve in the brake pipe that should have closed immediately did not, and all the vacuum in the reservoirs on the slip coach was destroyed at once. We stood there for ages. Nothing could be done until a locomotive was obtained, and could re-create the vacuum lost. It was fortunate that Bath goods depot, about a mile west of the passenger station, was still open and that there was a pilot engine on duty. Naturally, it could not come at once, and we sat out there for the best part of half an hour!

The Great Western used a very efficient and sophisticated form of the vacuum brake. It was always said that in pre-grouping days – even between the wars – the GWR invariably found a way of doing things differently from everyone else. So it was with the vacuum brake. When William Dean succeeded Joseph Armstrong as Locomotive, Carriage and Wagon Superintendent, in 1877, the GWR was using the Sanders & Bolitho form of the vacuum brake; but Dean was not satisfied with its performance, and he deputed Armstrong's third son, also named Joseph, to examine it, and make improvements. A young engineer not long arrived at Swindon from

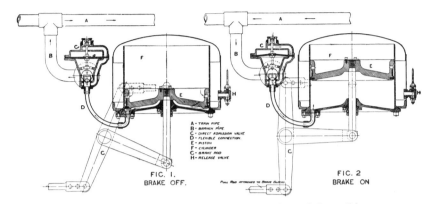

A - TRAIN PIPE
B - BRANCH PIPE
C - DIRECT ADMISSION VALVE
D - FLEXIBLE CONNECTION.
E - PISTON
F - CYLINDER
G - BRAKE ROD
H - RELEASE VALVE

FIG. I.
BRAKE OFF.

PULL ROD ATTACHED TO BRAKE BLOCKS

FIG. 2
BRAKE ON

Vacuum Brake Apparatus (*From the GWR General Appendix*)

the South Devon Railway, G. J. Churchward, no less, was assigned to assist Armstrong – 'Young Joe' as he was always known on the GWR – and the two of them together set out to increase the power of the brake. To avoid the use of larger cylinders Armstrong sought to improve things by exhausting the train pipe to a higher degree of vacuum. Now atmospheric pressure is about $14\frac{3}{4}$ lb/sq in, and if the system was exhausted to a perfect vacuum, this would be the maximum pressure available for braking. Such a condition would of course not be practicable in ordinary railway conditions, but Young Joe felt he could get much nearer to it than was obtained with the Sanders & Bolitho brake.

In that brake, as in other forms of the vacuum type, a steam operated ejector was used for maintaining vacuum in the train pipe, and those then in use were not capable of maintaining more than about two-thirds of a perfect vacuum, about 20 inches of mercury or 10 lb/sq in. In earlier days, before the invention of the injector for feeding water into the boiler of a locomotive, reliance had been placed on a pump, driven off some part of the motion, and now Joe Armstrong conceived the idea of using a pump driven off one of the engine crossheads to create the vacuum required for the brake. It was extremely successful, and enabled a vacuum of 26 or 27 inches to be maintained when the locomotive was running. Moreover, it had the great advantage of being independent of the steam pressure in the boiler. He designed a form of crosshead pump that became standard on all Swindon built locomotives until the very end of Great Western steam. It provided some 50 per cent greater braking force for the same diameter of brake cylinder as with the ejector

42

maintained vacuum brake system on other railways. Of course it was not operative when the engine was stationary, and a separate ejector was necessary to blow off the brakes from a standing start; but once the train was on the move it came powerfully into operation when needed.

I must however tell of one occasion when Joe Armstrong's brake, or rather the maintenance of it, did let the party down. I had an engine pass to ride the Penzance–Wolverhampton express through from Plymouth to Birmingham. It was just after the restoration of that service, in the autumn of 1945, and having seen Star class engines on the long through working between Newton Abbot and Wolverhampton I hoped to get one on the occasion when I travelled. We certainly had one, *Princess Charlotte*, on the Cornish section of the train, running non-stop from Plymouth to Exeter, but when we reached Exeter, the addition of the Paignton and Torquay section of the train brought the load up to 473 tons and the through engine to go forward to Wolverhampton was No 5015 *Kingswear Castle*, based at Stafford Road. The driver and fireman looked anything but pleased at having a visitor on the footplate, and we had not gone far with this very heavy load before it was very obvious they were in the dumps. There was a leak somewhere in the brake system, and the crosshead pump could not create enough vacuum to keep the brakes off on this great 15-coach train. They were having to use the big ejector as well. Normally this was used only at starting, and its continuous use took a considerable amount of the steam that could have been more profitably used for hauling that long train.

Before we had gone far it was evident that we were going to lose a fair amount of time. Continuous use of the big ejector, and the weight of that train was causing such a drain on the steam supply that we began to lose pressure in the boiler. But the ejector had to be kept on, because that leak in the vacuum system meant that the crosshead pump would not have been enough to keep the brakes from leaking on, and then we should be stranded. It was better to struggle on at far below scheduled speed than to try and make faster time. The Newton Abbot inspector who was riding with me threw out a message as we passed through Cullompton asking for a running shed fitter to meet us when we reached Taunton. We managed, just, to struggle over Whiteball summit, and ran smartly enough down Wellington bank; but on arrival at Taunton, after a pretty thorough examination, the fitter could find no defect that he could remedy. The driver felt we would have lost less time in the long run by struggling on to Bristol, whence we would have to have been double headed in any case with such a load over the severe gradients of the line north; but the inspector commandeered a new County class 4–6–0 that was ready to hand, and left *Kingswear Castle* as a casualty at Taunton.

Developments of the vacuum brake on the GWR did not end with the adoption of Joe Armstrong's inventions. In the early 1900s Churchward was conscious that despite the use of a higher degree of vacuum than that used on other railways its capacity for stopping was inferior to that of the Westinghouse air brake. He put one of the most inventive of his draughtsmen, Conrad K. Dumas, on to the job of getting quicker and more effective action of the vacuum brake. Dumas, who later earned great distinction as an experimental engineer, and was later involved in most important testing work with the Swindon dynamometer car, fastened on to one feature of the continuous automatic brakes in use in Great Britain that was common to both vacuum and compressed air working, namely the time lag in application between the front and rear of a train. Action was initiated at the driver's brake valve, in the locomotive cab, and it was propagated down the length of the train. With the vacuum brake, all air for reducing or completely destroying the vacuum in the train had to pass through the driver's brake valve; with the so-called direct admission valve, invented by Dumas, two of which were fitted on each coach, atmospheric air was admitted to the train pipe at a large number of intermediate points, and the time of full application of the brake throughout the train was reduced to less than half its former value. After initial trials it was adopted as standard for all GWR passenger rolling stock from 1913 onwards, and it made the vacuum brake as used on Great Western trains equal in application performance to the compressed air brake, as then used by certain lines in Great Britain, particularly the LBSCR, GER and Caledonian.

Reverting to the practice of slip-coach working, and anticipating in one respect the subject matter of my next chapter, Churchward's responsibility for coaching stock as well as locomotives led him to an interesting investigation into the rolling resistance of passenger vehicles, which had eventually a very amusing climax. Early dynamometer car trials confirmed that while Churchward's new locomotives had ample power to pull in terms of effort at the drawbar, the standard coaching stock of the Dean type, with their clerestory roofs and handsome external finish seemed to have a rolling resistance that was high in relation to the tare weight. Results that had been obtained with the little four-wheeled dynamometer car of the London & North Western Railway suggested that the Wolverton built stock mostly with low elliptical roof profile was considerably better than that of Swindon. In those days such conditions as the external smoothing of the coach bodies did not enter into it. At the usual running speeds of about 60mph it would have made very little difference anyway. Churchward set his carriage design staff to an examination of the methods of suspension, 'below stairs' as it were, and particularly the form of axle-box and its lubrication. As a result, a great improvement was made, although the inclusion of many Dean clerestory coaches in the make-up of the principal expresses was still making the trains as a whole pull more heavily than those of the LNWR.

Then someone, I cannot remember who, suggested that coach resistance would be further reduced by use of an early form of roller bearings. It may have been one of the Board members who had an interest in this development. Churchward was sceptical, and having great confidence in the new type of axle-box he was using, with a very efficient form of oil lubrication for the plain bearings, he determined upon a practical demonstration. There was no need to go to the trouble of a dynamometer car test to measure the pull. In any case he fitted up only one of the latest 70ft corridor coaches with roller bearings. Where the demonstration was staged I do not know, but it was a length of line on which two coaches, one with plain and one with roller bearings, could be loose shunted and have room to roll freely. Artful could well have been Churchward's second name! He had the two coaches marshalled together, but uncoupled, first with the roller bearing one leading. The pair were then propelled up to a speed of between 30 and 40mph, and then let go. They remained closely together until coming to a stop. Then they were re-arranged with the plain bearing coach leading, and the loose-shunt repeated. The leading coach went sailing ahead, leaving the roller bearing one far behind, and that was the end of roller bearings, so far as Churchward was concerned!

4

Seven Ages of GWR Coaches

Although my awareness of Great Western locomotives and coaching stock can be traced back to 1907 I do not think my appreciation of their well-nigh endless variety began until 1913, when I was presented with a Gauge 1 model of the 4-4-0 locomotive No 3410 *Sydney*, and three clerestory roofed bogie coaches, painted in the historic chocolate and cream livery. I am old enough just to remember having seen some coaches in that style, but in 1913 it had been completely superseded by a rich Tuscan red, still plentifully lined out in gold. It was not until very many years later that I realised that my model train included a vehicle that had no actual prototype. Readers who have access to the files of *The Locomotive Magazine* will find on the very last page of the 1907 volume a photograph of a GWR Bogie Brake Van, and like the other two vehicles in that train of mine it had a clerestory roof. But for once Bassett-Lowke had slipped up, for no such vehicle was ever built by the GWR. They had plenty of full brake vans running in conjunction with the clerestory roofed coaches, but they were of the much flatter roofed type, sometimes called the three-curve roof, consisting of a slightly curved portion over most of the width, and then a sharp curve at each side leading down to the cantrail.

My three Gauge 1 coaches were in lithographed tin plate, most realistic, and non-corridor; but in the real corridor version I travelled many times. If one could, they were to be avoided at times of peak traffic. The thirds seated three aside comfortably, but four only at a squash, and the seat reservation people cheerfully booked four aside. I well remember a journey on the 3.30pm from Paddington just before the August Bank Holiday of 1925, when uncertainty in my arrangements had not enabled me to book a seat until five days previously, and the best they could do was an inside seat in a corridor clerestory third. It rode well enough at speeds up to nearly 80mph but we were all terribly cramped inside, and it was not until we reached Torquay that some of my fellow passengers got out.

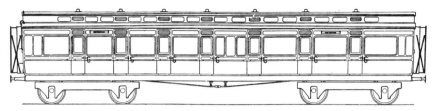
Dean's corridor composite coach of 1900 design

Statistically these coaches were admirable, carrying 2.67 passengers per ton of tare weight, and of course they were most attractive to behold and photograph, but that passenger-weight ratio was something of a snare and delusion when it came to weighing up the locomotive effort needed to pull them. As I mentioned in the previous chapter, tests with Churchward's dynamometer car revealed that the drawbar pull per ton of tare weight was much higher than the London & North Western Railway measured with trains of contemporary stock built at Wolverton.

Quite apart from any memories of crowded holiday journeys those corridor clerestories have always remained among my greatest favourites of pre-grouping passenger coaches. Of course, when I first noticed them in any detail they were in red, and carrying scarlet roof boards, but when the change back to chocolate and cream came in 1922, I was glad to see that the old clerestories were not excluded, and at first the lining out was as elaborate as ever. When the time came for my large Gauge O model railway to be dismantled in 1979, with no more than a few specially favourite items to be kept to adorn a purely static exhibit in the bungalow we designed to suit our advancing years, one coach that I still have is a Dean 57ft corridor composite, which aptly represents the glory of the Great Western in the early 1900s, and in the revival of the chocolate and cream style as I remembered it, and travelled in it in the 1920s. The Gauge 1 coaches that I had as a boy were, alas, long since disposed of; but so far as brake and luggage vans were concerned the formation of trains like the Cornishman at the turn of the century had brake-thirds, with clerestory roofs, rather than the flatter roofed full brakes.

In the previous chapter of this book I have referred to the development in axle-box design that Churchward instigated in his drive towards providing increased accommodation for passengers with a reduced rolling resistance of the vehicles. But the second age

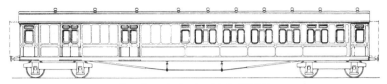
Dreadnought brake third of 1904

of Great Western coaches was about to come into being, to shock the traditionalists both on the railway, and in the ranks of its devoted amateur admirers. When he first proposed to build coaches of 68ft overall length, with clipper bodies bulging out to 9ft 6in overall width it was the signal engineer who raised objections. Now A. T. Blackall, who had held the office from 1897, was a chief officer of the Company, and like Churchward he then reported direct to the Board. When the proposal for 68 and 70ft coaches was first made he was concerned because the increased distance between the bogies would allow the facing-point lock fouling bars to be uncovered by the wheel flanges momentarily and could give rise to unsafe conditions. Churchward said nothing at the time, but before the next Board meeting, without a word to Blackall, he had the total number of locking bars checked on the routes where he proposed to use the new coaches. Because of their size they were in any case restricted in use generally to former broad gauge routes. He then estimated that the cost of lengthening them would be a mere £5,000, and when the question came up again at the next Board, and he told them of this estimate, Blackall was promptly told to get on with the job of altering them.

The first of the new 68ft coaches, diners with high elliptical roofs and clipper-sided bodies were ready in time to be run on the Cornish Riviera Express when it was introduced in July 1904, and it must be admitted that in an otherwise uniform rake of Dean clerestory coaches those huge composite dining cars had a most unprepossessing look. Connoisseurs said they spoilt the look of the train; but Churchward was already used to being told he was spoiling the look of things and in 1905, when a complete rake of the large new coaches was put on to the Cornish Riviera Express they were much criticised. It was not so much the look of the vehicles, but that they did not have separate doors for each compartment. The complaints were really quite hypothetical. It was stressed that with end doors only there would be wild confusion at stations with one crowd of passengers surging in to meet, head-on in the corridors, another crowd struggling to get out. The new coaches had certainly been made very wide, so wide indeed that like the diners they could be used only on those routes that had previously been broad gauge where advantage could be taken of the wider structural clearances. But as the 'Dreadnought' stock, as it became known from the then new battleships of the Royal Navy, was confined to the Cornish Riviera Express running non-stop between Paddington and Plymouth the suggestion of wild melees between ingoing and outgoing passengers at every station stop was the product of a too-vivid imagination.

A more cogent argument against the Dreadnoughts was their limited route availability. When the time came for them to be displaced from the Cornish Riviera Express, around 1914, they could not be used except on West of England trains. Their extreme overall width of 9ft 6in precluded their use on the direct South Wales expresses, taking the Badminton route and through the Severn Tunnel. In these coaches however, despite their recessed doors and lack of external streamlining, Churchward had notably reduced the rolling resistance compared with that of the Dean clerestories. On a dynamometer car test carried out on the Cornish Riviera Express in 1908 the drawbar pull exerted by the four-cylinder 4–6–0 engine *Dog Star* in sustaining 70mph on level track with a load of 290 tons showed a tractive resistance of about $13\frac{1}{2}$ lb/ton at that speed, which is almost the same as given by the Johansen formula evolved for standard LMS coaching stock about 1930. In that train tested in 1908 all vehicles would have been of the Dreadnought type except for the dynamometer car, which had a clerestory roof with sloping ends as used on the Great Western royal train, and for the Taunton clerestory slip coach. A Dreadnought could not have been conveyed on the Ilfracombe line.

Unfavourable reaction to the Dreadnoughts both within and without the railway service led to the building, in 1906–7, of some even longer vehicles, the first of the famous 70ft stock, but with overall width reduced to 9ft. These huge vehicles had the individual doors for each compartment restored, but in order not to encroach upon the loading gauge on lines built to standard rather than broad gauge side clearances all the body-side doors were recessed to an amount sufficient to keep the handles within the 9ft maximum overall width. They were designed for maximum passenger accom-modation and the thirds seated no fewer than 80, for a tare weight of only 33 tons. They were clearly designed with the holiday traffic to South Devon and Cornwall in mind, but no less perhaps

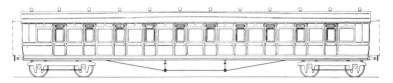

'Concertina' corridor third of 1906

for South Wales. Great Western men have more than once told me that on an all-the-year-round basis the passenger service between Paddington, Newport, Cardiff and Swansea was the most profitable on the system. The external appearance of these carriages, arising from the succession of recessed doors gave rise to the nickname of 'concertinas'. They were curious carriages to ride in; if one had a window corner seat and it was necessary to give plenty of elbow-room for a broad-gauge fellow passenger, one had to tuck in tight where the window seat extended farther out than the door. I did not like the concertinas much better than the Dreadnoughts. There was a fine colour plate of one of the concertinas in the celebrated part-work *Our Home Railways* published in 1908.

When it comes to the question of coach colours, other than the historic chocolate and cream, the Great Western set its historians some teasing problems. From the very moment that Churchward took office, in 1902, he seems to have set out to produce a simpler coach livery and he began by painting some vehicles in a plain brown, with gold lining. The famous F. Moore series of coloured postcards includes one of a seven-coach Dreadnought set on the up Cornish Riviera Express hauled by the *Knight of the Grand Cross* near Acton in this plain brown style, though in my own boyhood at Reading, when I was a season-ticket holder between there and Mortimer, the darker, richer, Tuscan red had become standard. When newly painted the roofs were *white*, but as can well be imagined they did not stay like that for very long. Another interesting feature was the monogram, with the scroll letters GWR entwined, a relic of the days of Dean. Then, about the time the concertinas were introduced a much more splendid display was adopted. This took the two shields from the coat of arms and encircled them with a garter and much ornamentation, and then added the crests of London and Bristol each about 3ft to the left and right of the central device. The gartered insignia was also used on the tenders and tank sides of locomotives instead of the entwined scroll letters. The winged crest of the City of London, and the cross-arms of

Bristol which had been used to adorn some of the Dean 7ft 8in 4–2–2s were not used again on locomotives but the three-part coach decoration was continued when the chocolate and cream livery was restored in 1922.

There was an amusing sequel to this in 1927, when the new 'super' four-cylinder 4–6–0 was introduced. These were originally intended to be known as the Cathedral class, and at Swindon the 'secret' became such an open one that the news got into the local Wiltshire newspapers. Then, in view of the intention to send the first of the new engines to the USA, and that it would, in effect, represent the railways of Great Britain at the centenary celebrations of the Baltimore & Ohio Railroad, permission was obtained from Buckingham Palace to name the engine *King George V*. As completed and sent to America it carried the gartered insignia on the tender, flanked by the words GREAT WESTERN as many hundreds of Swindon built locomotives also did at that time; but *King George V* came in for more than the usual amount of scrutiny, and eventually that gartered insignia came to the notice of the College of Heralds, which pointed out that the surrounding garter was quite illegal, heraldically. The garter was quietly dropped on engines and coaches, and for a time the Company's official device, with the crests surmounting the shields, was substituted, later to be succeeded by the very plain sans-serif GWR in a circle.

The building of the concertinas was only the first phase of what can be termed the third age of 20th century coach design on the Great Western. None other than 70-footers were built, of which the tricomposite slip coaches were perhaps the most distinctive. The original Cornish Riviera rake of 1904 included a tri-composite clerestory brake, for Falmouth. Second class did not finally disappear from the Great Western until 1910. In the end it was really more trouble than it was worth, because the basic fare was only $1\frac{1}{4}$d ($\frac{1}{2}$p) per mile, against a penny a mile third class. When new coaches were needed on routes where the 70 footers could not be used the very handsome 57ft toplight stock was introduced. These also were 9ft wide overall, but the doors were not recessed, and the appearance was greatly improved in consequence. Their nickname arose from the oblong hammered-glass toplights above the windows. Introduced first in 1907 they became the standard main line express carriage for about 15 years. A 70ft toplight version was introduced on to the South Wales and Paddington–Birkenhead trains, and replaced the Dreadnoughts on

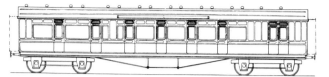

Toplight brake composite of pre World War I

the Cornish Riviera Express in 1914.

The toplight coaches stood out as an epitome of Edwardian elegance in British passenger coaching stock design, though internally, like the concertinas, maximum accommodation for a minimum of tare weight was always a major consideration. At first the bodies were of timber, built on a steel underframe, and I shall always remember the colour vividly from an incident after the Reading accident of 1914, when a race special which had stopped at the up main platform started away, against signals, and drew out to the main line just as the 9am Worcester to Paddington express was running through. One of my school friends came in a day or so later with a souvenir of the crash, a shattered piece of panelling from the leading coach of the express still carrying the fine rich colouring of that era. When the change to steel panelling began in 1914, although there were no mouldings above the waistline the lining out was retained, in the same style as though the mouldings were still there. The Cornish Riviera Express as I saw it going through Reading looked magnificent with its new coaches, while at that time the 3.30pm from Paddington, also a 3-hour Exeter non-stop, was usually made up of concertinas.

My day-to-day acquaintance with the Great Western ceased in the late autumn of 1914, when my parents moved to a house in Reading itself, and I no longer had to travel daily by train to school; it was not until 1921 that I saw its trains again. The red livery for the coaches still prevailed, but the locomotives were in their wartime plain green, unlined, and many, even those on the principal express trains looked quite drab. In 1922, at the undoubted instigation of Sir Felix Pole, a start was made with restoration of the chocolate and cream livery; but it was no more than gradual, and even as late as the summer of 1924, while all the regular express train rakes had been repainted, when extra coaches were added at times of additional traffic they were often maroon toplights or concertinas. As they were added in front of the regular sets they spoiled the uniform appearance of the trains, much to the disgust of photographers, who recorded one or two dingy coaches,

52

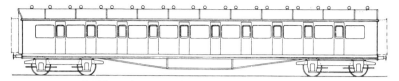
A 70ft corridor third for South Wales services, 1922

needing a wash, interposed between a none-too-clean plain green engine and the gleaming chocolate and cream set bringing up the rear. I took a number of photographs myself from the old A excursion platform at Paddington, in 1922 and 1923, and am astonished at the mixture of stock that these old prints now reveal.

It was in the summer of 1923 that the fourth age of Great Western corridor coaching stock began, with the introduction of the new smooth-sided steel panelled trains, first for the South Wales service. Like their predecessors they were 70ft long and 9ft wide, but toplights for the windows were not included, and the sides were devoid of any moulding effect. The lined appearance of the old raised mouldings was retained, however, in the painting, but a technical innovation was the use of buck-eye couplers within the seven-coach train sets. The brake-thirds at each end were equipped so that they could be coupled to vehicles having the conventional standard screw couplings. They were considerably heavier than the toplights and concertinas weighing between 37 and 38 tons tare. The South Wales seven-coach sets included two brake-thirds, two 10-compartment thirds, two first/third composites, and a composite dining car; when production continued to provide vehicles for the new type of the Cornish and Birmingham services, brake-composites were needed for the various through carriages included in trains like the Cornish Riviera Express. During the summer of 1924 the standard formation of this latter train was five of the new coaches, including dining car, for Penzance, and brake composites for St Ives, Falmouth, and Plymouth. Slip coaches for Taunton and Exeter were not carried during the height of the summer, and the Weymouth portion had a slip coach of the toplight type.

The first time I photographed the up Limited leaving Penzance, in 1924, a 57ft toplight still in red was marshalled next to the engine, a dingy Mogul. There was certainly plenty of variety to be seen in the coaches leaving Penzance that morning. The immediately succeeding Liverpool and Manchester express included a beautifully clean London & North Western three-coach set of the largest elliptical-roofed Wolverton stock, still in pre-grouping colours; as far as the Great Western was concerned the best looking train was the 10.30am for Wolverhampton, with a new 57ft steel-sided set, headed by a freshly out-shopped Mogul, looking as smart as a plain green GWR engine could. It was when these Cornish trains proceeded eastwards and picked up a variety of through carriages that the uniformity of their make-up was lost. I photographed the 11am up from Penzance at Southcote Junction one day in the early summer of 1924, and the formation, front to rear, was toplight brake third; toplight composite; clerestory composite; concertina brake composite; Dreadnought dining car; four-coach set from Penzance, including concertina brake third; toplight composite, concertina composite, and toplight brake third. Could that be beaten for variety in the same train!

The West of England postal special leaving Penzance at 6pm, each evening carried an intriguing variety of stock. When photographing it many times during a holiday in Cornwall in 1924 I was far more concerned with the locomotives, because it was the only train west of Truro that was usually hauled by a 4–6–0, from Exeter shed. But when re-examining those old pictures I realised that the two train sets were not alike. On the 6pm up one set had a three-curve non-clerestory 40ft van next to the engine, still in red-brown, whereas the other had a 54ft clerestory van, with side-positioned gangways to couple with the 70ft elliptical roofed TPO van which was marshalled second in the train. Unlike its famous counterpart on the Euston–Aberdeen run the West of England postal train was not turned at journey's end, and as the exchange of mail bags at speed was carried out on both eastbound and westbound journeys there had to be mail pickup and set down apparatus on both sides, though not on the same vehicle. In 1924 the 70ft TPO van second from the engine had the apparatus on the up side. Its use diminished in the years between the wars, because of the availability of rapid road transport from major postal centres, and when the TPO service was re-instated after the second world war the apparatus was worked only at Liskeard on the eastbound journey. It was still busily employed on the down run, and after it was restored and I was living at Chippenham I used occasionally take a walk to watch the operation, around midnight.

For a railway whose engineering was so conservative in other respects Great Western coach design seemed to change with unusual rapidity. The latest form of 70 footers had been in service for little more than five years, before a new version was introduced.

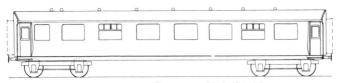

Centenary third of 1935

They definitely had the 'look' of the fourth age, but were shorter and wider, 61ft 4in by 9ft 7in. A significant change from previous practice was the relative high tare weight per passenger, because the eight-compartment thirds, seating 64, had a weight of 34.1 tons. An especially notable feature was the high proportion of third to first class accommodation. While the brake-composites detached for St Ives, Falmouth, and Plymouth seated 12 firsts and 32 thirds, in the Penzance portion, apart from dining cars there were seats for 184 thirds and only 24 firsts. The dining accommodation seated 95 thirds and 24 firsts at one sitting. A novel feature for the Great Western was the inclusion of a separate 42.6 ton kitchen car. A total of eight coaches was taken through to Penzance, and these, with the St Ives, Falmouth, and Plymouth coaches made a total tare weight of 378 tons to be taken over the severe gradients of the South Devon line. The official limit for a King class engine to take unassisted between Newton Abbot and Plymouth was 360 tons, so that with the full 11-coach summer load drivers would be entitled to stop for a bank engine; but if all was going well on the footplate most of the crews preferred to carry on. I had a fine trip at Easter 1935 when the train was running in two sections, and the first part carried 376 tons beyond Exeter, and engine No 6016 *King Edward V*, climbed Dainton and Rattery inclines in excellent style.

Nevertheless, 1935 was the centenary year of the GWR and it was decreed that there should be yet another change of rolling stock on the Cornish Riviera Express. The 61ft 4in by 9ft 7in stock of 1929 had the same route restrictions as the old Dreadnoughts, and that designed for centenary year was the same, except that it re-introduced a feature that made the Dreadnoughts so unpopular, namely end doors only. By then, though, the LMS was setting the pace in coaching stock design, and what was deplored on the GWR in 1905 was acclaimed as highly commendable in 1935 except for those large single pane compartment windows. While they were grand for seeing the countryside they were the very devil when it came to ventilation. At first the entire expanse of window was in one sheet, opened by a drop type of fitting. Now if there is anything in the British compartment type of carriage more prone to create friction between passengers it is the ventilation, and how far the windows should be open. Those in the window corner seats would want the windows fairly well down, while their fellow passengers would be in a hurricane! The Riviera Centenary stock, as first introduced, was worse than anything that had gone before. The LMS design with fixed windows and horizontally sliding ventilators at the top were much better since with small wind-break flaps at the end of the sliding panes at the open end, the ventilators could be slid open to a pre-determined position which prevented draughts. This pattern was adopted on the centenary coaches in 1938. Even so they caused an occasional fracas.

It was very interesting to see how the provision for first and third class passenger accommodation was varying with the years, and how increasing luxury was steadily increasing the tare weight per passenger. The centenary thirds had only seven compartments, 56 passengers for a tare weight of 32 tons, with the ratio down to 1.75 compared with 2.5 in the concertinas. The brake composites forming the St Ives and Falmouth portions seated 12 firsts and 24 thirds, but, excluding the two rear coaches for Weymouth, which were slipped at Heywood Road Junction, the rest of the train seated 224 thirds and only 24 firsts, apart from dining accommodation. Considerable economies had been made in dining car weight, and instead of the very heavy 42 ton kitchen car of 1929 there was a combined kitchen and first class saloon (24 seats) weighing 33 tons, and a third class saloon seating 64. Apart from the Weymouth section, the 11 coaches conveyed beyond Heywood Road Junction had a tare weight just about equal to the 360-ton maximum for a King over the South Devon hills, though in the height of the summer extras were frequently added.

When the Bristolian was first put on in the autumn of 1935 it had six coaches of the 1929 Riviera stock, and a buffet car, but in 1936 the sixth age of Great Western corridor coach design began, with the so-called 'sunshine' type of 60ft vehicles, with wide windows, and deep metal framed ventilators with hinged vanes following LMS practice designed to deflect direct draughts. They were 9ft 0in wide, and thus capable of use on any GWR routes. The interiors, though not so spacious as on the Riviera Centenary stock, were very comfortable, and the picture windows gave an excellent lookout, as I found several times when stop-watching the up Bristolian. The thirds seated 64 passengers, and the tare weight of the complete seven-coach train on that service, in 1936–9, was 232 tons.

Generally these sunshine coaches were a very close copy, externally, of contemporary and slightly earlier Stanier stock on the LMS, and I shall always remember the disdain with which one of my friends at Euston spoke of them. He said: 'They've copied ours, including all the faults and none of the virtues!' In those years however I was not travelling much on the Great Western except for business between Paddington, Chippenham and Bristol and so had little opportunity to sample them in holiday traffic conditions.

During the war years I had many opportunities of sampling all vintages of Great Western stock. On many services, particularly the West to North trains from Bristol via the Severn Tunnel there were no such things as set rakes. Any vehicle that was roadworthy, GW or not, was pressed into service on that route and packed with passengers until it was bulging at the seams. I travelled north once in an ex-Midland Railway clerestory roofed brake-third of Bain vintage, the only place where I could find a seat, and all was reasonably well until our Castle got going north of Llanvihangel summit; there were times when I wondered if the old thing would hang together till we got to Hereford! However Great Western coaches were not immune from rough riding. Having to travel from Darlington to Glasgow one evening in 1936, I joined the 1.20pm Scotsman from Kings Cross and travelled in characteristic East Coast luxury to Edinburgh, at Waverley transferring to the connecting Glasgow train, which included a through GWR 57ft toplight brake composite from Southampton. Intrigued, I entrained in this coach. We did not break any speed records on that level run across to Glasgow, but I shall never forget the rough ride that old Great Western coach gave us. Everything about its bogies and suspension would seem to have been wrong!

After the war, with F. W. Hawksworth as Chief Mechanical Engineer, an entirely new design of main line passenger coach was evolved at Swindon, and at one stage I became personally involved. They were to be 64ft overall, with sloping roof-ends in the LNER style, and deep windows like the sunshine stock. The building programme for 1946 provided for 260 new coaches to be built, at a rate of one a week, but then human frailties intervened. Within Swindon Works a dispute between two unions as to who should do what brought production to a standstill. Deadlock prevailed, and to secure delivery of the urgently needed coaches a contract was placed with the Gloucester Railway Carriage & Wagon Company, and it in turn placed a contract for the vacuum brake equipment

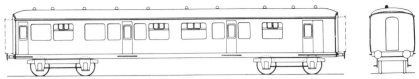

Hawksworth brake composite of post World War II years

with Westinghouse. I was then Chief Draughtsman of the Brake Department of the Company, and from the Gloucester RC&W Co I was informed that the equipment must be to the GWR standard pattern – naturally enough.

Now an outsider might have imagined that the vacuum brake was the vacuum brake, and that was all there was to it; but as related in the previous chapter, and particularly in its references to Joe Armstrong, it will have been appreciated that the vacuum brake on the GWR was something special. This was no more than vaguely sensed at Chippenham, and Gloucester, to whom we were contractors for the job, did not have a clue about the detail. It was agreed that we should approach Swindon direct, and while it was understood that things were a bit tense in the carriage works the drawing office was friendliness itself. F. C. Mattingley was then Chief Draughtsman, and he passed me over to his chief assistant for carriages and wagons, J. W. Innes, who had been principally concerned in the design of the new stock. He handed over to me a complete set of their drawings of cylinders, and the very important direct admission valves, two of which were mounted on each coach, and which made the very rapid action of the GWR version of the vacuum brake possible. I thanked him, and returned to Chippenham to study the drawings with my production colleagues in the works, and it soon became apparent that a good deal was left to the imagination on these drawings.

We drew up a fairly long list of queries and I went to see Innes a second time. The points raised were all vital to a firm manufacturing the equipment for the first time. But as we began to go through these items it was soon clear that the Swindon drawing office were as much in the dark as we were! It reminded me of the story E. L. Ahrons told of his early days on the GWR when there were no drawings of the old broad gauge 8ft 4–2–2s, and that in Armstrong's time it was a stock job on the locomotive side of the drawing office to make such drawings as they could, when there was no more urgent work on hand. To most of my queries Innes just did not know the answer, and we thus went down into the works to consult the foreman in charge of the vacuum brake section. Many of the details of construction, and especially the shop techniques for fitting up the special GWR form of cylinder, had been evolved over the years without any reference to the drawing office. Innes and his assistants learned as much about their own vacuum brake apparatus as we, at Westinghouse, did during this particular exercise.

The new coaches were naturally rather slow in coming off the production lines, and the Great Western Railway had become the Western Region of BR before they began to make much of an impact. But they came to be accepted as the best riding that had ever taken the road out of Paddington, and when the high speed Bristolian was restored in 1954 the stock was exclusively of the Hawksworth type. When I recorded a maximum speed of $102\frac{1}{2}$mph descending Dauntsey bank, behind engine No 6018 *King Henry VI* the riding in one of the rearward coaches of the train was quite perfect. In those post-war years there was little chance to marshal trains into uniform sets of equivalent vintage, and the seven-coach Bristolian was one of the few exceptions; but in the very mixed rakes of those troubled uncertain years, providing there were seats in it I always made for one of the Hawksworths.

5
Signals and Signalling Men

It has often been said that the Great Western Railway had a flair for doing things differently from everyone else; if it was not in actual equipment and working then it was in basic administration. In chapter 2 I referred to the way in which the senior executive officers at one time reported direct to the Board, rather than to the General Manager, and at the turn of the century this put the Signal Engineer in a position that was, I believe, unique in the profession at that time. Until the time of the conversion of the gauge, and for a short time afterwards, Thomas Blackall was assistant to the Chief Engineer for provision and maintenance of signalling equipment, the actual work being done locally by the Divisional Engineers. But Blackall himself retired in 1893, and responsibility for signalling was taken over by the Locomotive Department, under William Dean, with Blackall's son as assistant, and based at Reading. This unusual arrangement however lasted for no more than four years, and in 1897 A. T. Blackall was appointed Signal Engineer, as an independent chief officer of the company; six years later he took over responsibility for the Telegraph Department as well.

In Chapter 1 I mentioned the continued use of a white light as the 'all right' indication at night, when Charles Doncaster was at school at Reading in the 1890s; under A. T. Blackall all this was very quickly changed, and in 1900 in his classic work *Mechanical Railway Signalling,* H. Raynar Wilson published drawings of the complete new range of GWR semaphore signals, all using a green light as the 'all right' colour, and commenting: 'One of the, if not *the* most perfectly signalled railways in Great Britain is the Great Western . . .'. This was praise indeed; for that time the semaphores were very large and clearly presented, with a noticeable feature in the very sharp angle to which they lowered in the 'clear' position. The official angle was 60 degrees below horizontal (compared with 45 degrees of most other companies), but from a study of many photographs taken in the 1900–5 period it would often have seemed to be nearer 75 degrees. This may have been a relic of earlier practice when the arms were separate from the spectacle glasses, and worked in a slot in the post. The setting of the new arms could well have reflected the work of local signal inspectors, who at first were following old traditions.

As early as 1905 however it was evident that in other respects the Great Western was stepping into the very forefront of developing British signalling practice. Before the 19th century was out rapid progress was being made in the USA in methods of actuating the movement of semaphore signals and points by various forms of power. The railways there were neither so completely equipped as our own, nor were the safety regulations so comprehensive. In fact, the railways of the USA then had a very bad accident record, but in the actual mechanics of operating the signals and points they were in advance, so much so that the well established British signalling firms that had made such a major contribution to the very fine record of safe operation sustained in Great Britain were, around the 1900s, busy establishing trading associations, not only in the USA but with leading Continental manufacturers. The Great Western first put in a plant of the Siemens-Halske all-electric type at Didcot North Junction. It controlled two junctions on the line going north to Oxford and Banbury, the first that between the line from Didcot passenger station and the direct line from the Swindon direction, and the second, about $\frac{1}{4}$ mile further north with the through line passing clear of Didcot passenger station. The miniature-lever interlocking frame was of the standard Siemens pattern, and had 38 levers. The signals themselves were indistinguishable from the latest GWR type and had the electrical operating mechanism at the foot of the post.

At that time Blackall had two very able assistants, both of whom later succeeded to the office of Chief Signal & Telegraph Engineer. These were R. J. Insell, who was signalling assistant, and C. M. Jacobs, electrical assistant, and with experience of the Didcot installation it appeared to them that some of its features were unnecessarily complicated. It was then that the great project of completely rebuilding Snow Hill station at Birmingham was in hand, and thoughts naturally turned to power signalling. With co-operation between R. J. Insell and L. M. G. Ferreira, Engineer and Manager of the signal department of Siemens, a new version of the all-electric interlocking frame was designed. One of the most important changes from the one installed at Didcot was that the actual interlocking between the levers was effected by means of a tappet mechanism, in the British style, rather than by cams. In construction it was remarkable in being of pedestal form only $12\frac{1}{2}$ inches wide from back to front. This unique form of interlocking frame was ideally suited to the particular location and design of the signalbox itself. The two were so inter-related as to make one wonder if it was not another case of the proverbial 'chicken and egg' situation: which came first? At Birmingham North, to minimise cabin area on the ground, and still give the signalman a good view over all the tracks the cabin itself was mounted on a single line of steel stanchions. With such a supporting structure it was clearly desirable to keep the cabin itself as narrow as possible, and it was only 10ft wide inside. So, whether the cabin design came first, and the unique form of the locking frame was contrived to suit, or whether the design of the frame allowed for the unusual cabin structure is nowadays anyone's guess! In any case the combination was never repeated.

Messrs Insell and Ferreira had another innovation to spring upon the British signalling world in the early post-war years; before that, though, and while he was still assistant to Blackall, Insell had become one of the foremost British advocates of the three-position upper quadrant semaphore signal. It was largely at his instigation that a true American type of signal was installed in the most prominent and heavily worked signal location on the whole railway. It had a tubular steel post, a top-mast electric mechanism and the arm had red, yellow and green spectacle glasses. After passing under the great Bishops Road bridge all departure lines from Paddington, except from the Metropolitan line, funnelled into one for a short distance, and just ahead of this general confluence there was an advanced starting signal – in advance, as it were, of all the platform starters – and which every outgoing train had to pass. And it was at this location that the three-position upper quadrant signal was installed, in 1914. As far as I recall it remained there until the remodelling of the station layout in the early 1930s. This isolated example, on the main line, proved the forerunner of a complete installation on the Ealing & Shepherds Bush Railway, for which the Great Western did all the civil and electrical engineering, and the signalling. My old firm obtained the contract for the supply of the material and its installation, and in connection with this there is a story to be told 'out of school'. Like the advanced starting signal at Paddington the electrical mechanisms for the three-position signals were 'top-mast', and very heavy; one day the installation gang, working sky-high up a tubular mast, dropped one of them, to a monumental crash on the ballast. It was whispered in the office that the man responsible was the son of the Managing Director, then no more than a trainee!

Insell succeeded Blackall as Signal & Telegraph Engineer in 1923, and for a time it seemed that there was no end to the variety of the ways in which power signalling was being introduced on the GWR. In that same year he was elected President of the Institution of Railway Signal Engineers (IRSE), and for a man who had been so connected with innovations his Address to members was singularly free from points of controversy. At the very time he took office, again in collaboration with Ferreira, he was developing the system of route lever working which bore their joint names. After a small experimental installation at Winchester–Cheesehill, the last interlocking on the Didcot, Newbury & Southampton line before it joined the London & South Western main line at Shawford Junction, two relatively large plants were installed at Newport, Monmouthshire. In the larger of the two cabins, at the west end of the station, the locking frame had 144 levers, to operate 116 signals, 27 points and 3 controls. The miniature levers had four positions, registered by notches on the quadrants, designated N, C, T, S. To set up a route the lever was first moved from the N to the C position, whereupon the lighting of an indication lamp showed that all the track circuits concerned were clear. Then the lever was put to the T position, which caused all the points in the route to line up correctly; when this had occurred and all the points were locked, another indication lamp lit up and the lever was then free to be advanced to the final position, which operated the signal motor and lowered the arm.

In the proceedings of the Institution of Railway Signal Engineers it was left to another contractor rather than Insell himself to extol the virtues of this system; it may, or may not have been significant that Newport, other than the little plant at Cheesehill, remained the only one of its kind.

In addition to making a trial of the Westinghouse electro-pneumatic system in a small plant at Slough (Bath Road Junction) a very interesting arrangement of automatic intermediate signals was put in by Blackall on the main line between Tilehurst and Goring. The block sections there were 2.8 miles (Tilehurst to

Pangbourne) and 3¼ miles (Pangbourne to Goring), and the new intermediate signals on all four running lines were sited mid-way between the existing mechanical block posts. At ground level at each location there was a substantial steel case about 4 ft high on top of which was mounted the tubular steel mast which carried the semaphore signal. The arms were of standard Great Western pattern, lower quadrant, and it all looked very neat, with not even an operating rod showing; but open the door of that case and you were confronted by the most incredible jumble of cranks, rods, electro-magnets, and two sprocket wheels connected by a glorified bicycle chain.

Whether the equipment inside the case was actually purchased from America I do not know. They were installed as long ago as 1907. But it was a Union Switch and Signal Co, design, and looked for all the world like some hurriedly assembled laboratory hook-up. The 'Union', as it was always known at Westinghouse, was primarily an exponent of electro-pneumatic signalling, and it was so easy to produce a compressed-air cylinder to provide the upward thrust needed to move a semaphore arm from on to off. Arranging for an electric motor to do the same thing was not so simple. But around 1910 the gifted English designer under whom I worked for some years at Westinghouse, Walter Allan Pearce, gathered all those essential American bits and pieces together into a beautifully compact and efficient signal machine which lasted Westinghouse for as long as there were semaphore signals needing to be worked electrically. I had not long previously joined the firm when I became involved in an interesting example of their use on the Great Western.

Until the 1920s Newton Abbot station was an unwieldy agglomeration of tracks and platforms that had grown from the original broad gauge station built by Brunel for the South Devon Railway, incorporating his characteristic all-over roof. With the rapid growth in holiday traffic, and with it the importance of Newton Abbot as a place where the Cornish and Kingswear sections of many trains were divided, or combined, complete reconstruction of the station was agreed to provide four platform lines, of maximum length, and two through lines outside, for non-stopping trains. The use of very long platforms had been advantageous at Birmingham, Snow Hill, though not perhaps for the same purpose as envisaged at Newton Abbot, at which latter the dividing, or combining of lengthy express passenger trains was a

64

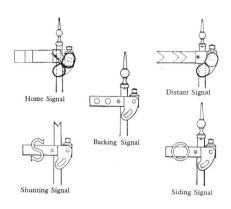

Home Signal

Distant Signal

Backing Signal

Shunting Signal

Siding Signal

Above: Great Western signals

Right: Box platform down starting signal,
slotted with distants for the war-time Farleigh
Down signalbox

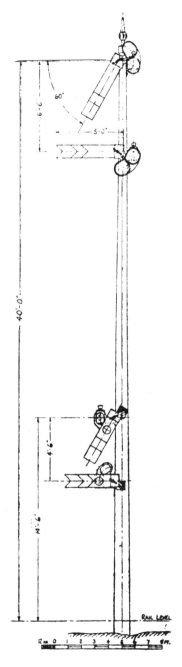

65

major consideration. As at Birmingham scissors crossovers were provided at the mid-point of some platforms, so that, for example an express from Plymouth and Cornwall could approach on the outer through line and cross to the eastern end of the up main platform while the Kingswear section, to be joined to it was already standing at the western end of the same platform. The new station was formally opened in April 1927.

In view of the variety of power signalling equipment already in use on the Great Western Railway those of us who were in the signalling business had looked forward and perhaps with some anxiety to what might transpire, and to whom what would probably be a very large contact would be awarded. The GWR already had a small frame of Westinghouse manufacture at Slough; there was the Birmingham type, and lastly the Insell–Ferreira route setting system at Newport. Although Insell himself was in the Chair at Reading it was unlikely that his former 'love', the three-position upper quadrant semaphore would be adopted, in view of the almost unanimous recommendation of the IRSE committee on three-position signalling that the signals themselves should be of the colour-light type. While it was disappointing to learn in due course that Newton Abbot was to be almost entirely mechanical, Westinghouse did get something out of it because the scissors crossovers in the middle of the station, and the semaphore signals reading over them were electrically worked through circuit controllers actuated by full sized levers in the main locking frames in East and West signalboxes. The S & T men at Reading chose the top-mast variety of Pearce's beautifully compact electric signal machine, and as everywhere else they gave very long and excellent service; indeed as these words are being written some survive at Newton Abbot but will be replaced when colour-light signals controlled from the new Exeter panel signalbox are commissioned probably by 1986, almost 60 years after installation.

One of the most important developments in the pre-war period was that of the audible cab signal, which originated about the turn of the century, in the first place to facilitate the running of trains in foggy weather. For some years it had been felt that the system of calling out fogmen, and of using detonators for warning trains was unwieldy, and that it led to many delays that might have been avoided. The original conception of an audible signal in the engine cab was due to the combined efforts of four young men in the early 1900s, three of them signal engineers, and the fourth a traffic man:

Insell himself; C. M. Jacobs, telegraph assistant; E. A. Bowden, a lecturer in signalling; and R. H. Nicholls, who many years later became Superintendent of the Line. At an early stage however it was felt that the automatic warning system should also include some measure of actual brake control, and accordingly the Locomotive Department was called into consultation. It is indeed interesting that one of the first technical descriptions of the system came not from any one of the four pioneers, but from none other than W. A. Stanier, in 1914 when he was Assistant Manager of the Locomotive Works at Swindon. The Institution of Mechanical Engineers had sponsored a meeting at which five short papers on Locomotive Cab Signals were to be presented, and Stanier, as a Member of the Institution described the Great Western system in a finely illustrated paper. He certainly acknowledged the assistance he had had from his signalling colleagues, and both Blackall and Insell took part in the subsequent discussion; but it was evident from his presentation of the paper, and his replies to a very full discussion that Stanier had the job very much at his fingertips.

The principles and operation of the GWR system of cab signalling, and automatic train control are so well known as to need no recapitulation here. In the early 1920s when the whole field of automatic train control was examined by a committee set up by the Ministry of Transport under the chairmanship of the Chief Inspecting Officer of Railways, Col Sir John Pringle, the system received general commendation, though at that time many interests outside the GWR did not feel it went far enough, in that the control was no more than intermittent, and was based entirely upon the indication given by the distant signal. The attention of the up and coming generation of young engineers in Westinghouse, for example, was constantly directed towards developments in the USA, on many important main lines of which legislation had been imposed requiring the installation of *continuous* automatic train control, with continuous visual indications in the locomotive cab. That the systems being evolved to meet these mandatory requirements were very complicated, and correspondingly expensive went without saying, while many British locomotive men expressed horror at the idea of drivers having to pay attention to a *visual* indication inside the cab when all their attention should be given to the road ahead.

I can, however, well remember the reaction of some of our own senior men to this attitude, which they regarded as reactionary, and a failure to face up to the needs of the future, but within the railway service itself there was guarded approval on the north-going lines of the principles of the Great Western system if not in the details of its accomplishment. The chief objection seemed to lie against the use of a contact ramp, for the pick up, though at first little was done towards developing any alternative. Meanwhile the Great Western was gradually extending the area over which its own system was applied, and in the early 1930s when Government funds to finance works for the relief of unemployment were made available, the Company took the opportunity to extend the system to cover the entire main line network. The number of new locomotive equipments required was far in excess of what could be manufactured in the signal works at Reading and at Swindon, and rather to the disgust of some of our American-minded executives we received an order for 1000 sets of the cab equipment, strictly in accordance with the Great Western drawings.

This was no more than the beginning. The really big works for the relief of unemployment, so far as the GWR was concerned, lay in the rebuilding of the stations at Bristol Temple Meads and Cardiff General, together with the re-arrangement of the approach lines to Paddington, and all three projects involved complete resignalling. By that time Sir Felix Pole had left the Great Western, and was firmly entrenched as Chairman of Associated Electrical Industries. One subsidiary of this vast group was Metropolitan Vickers–GRS the British associate of the General Railway Signal Co, of the USA. It specialised only in all-electric operation of signals and points, controlled from an interlocking machine different from anything that had previously been used on the Great Western. It had what was sometimes called a 'pistol grip' form of handle, which pulled out horizontally, but its special feature lay in the method of completion of the lever stroke. In the Westinghouse miniature lever type completion of the lever stroke actuating points was halted briefly at a check-lock position on the quadrant, until a lamp indication showed that the points had moved correctly and were locked in their new position. Then the signalman could move the lever to the completion of its stroke which released the interlocking to allow the signalman to operate the next lever in the sequence, for example to clear a related signal. In the GRS machine this last movement was done automatically. When the electrical indication had responded correctly a small electro-magnet was energised and the horizontal sliding lever was pushed to its final extent. The operation was known as 'dynamic-indication'. It had no particular merit over the alternative way. It was just another way of doing the same job.

It was perhaps no surprise in view of GRS being a part of Sir Felix Pole's vast empire that it received the contract for resignalling at Paddington, and then at Temple Meads; but two such large contracts were enough for one firm, and that for the almost equally large job at Cardiff was awarded to Westinghouse. Colour-light signalling was becoming the order of the day on all the British railways, but of course the Great Western had to do something different from everyone else. Insell had retired in 1928, and been succeeded as Signal & Telegraph Engineer by C. M. Jacobs, and it had been significant that neither of these senior assistants to A. T. Blackall had been members of the celebrated Three-Position Signal Committee of the Institution of Railway Signal Engineers. Insell's regard for the three-position upper quadrant semaphore had been well known. But in the signalling modernisation of the 1930s the Great Western disregarded entirely the recommendations of the IRSE and installed at all three major stations a system of colour-lights that reproduced by day exactly the same indications as had previously been given by the standard semaphores at night.

The so-called searchlight type of signal was used, having a relay mechanism in the signal head, and carrying miniature coloured roundels on the relay vane interposed in the light-beam system of the signal. When the relay was de-energised red was shown in a home signal, or yellow in a distant; when energised and the vane moved the colour changed to green. One searchlight signal unit could be mounted vertically above the other to provide the day colour-light equivalent of the familiar home and distant semaphore arm combination. In one respect these installations were standard, in that the enginemen had no new types of indication to learn, but they brought to the Great Western two new types of interlocking machine – the GRS with the pistol-grip handles and dynamic indication, and the latest Westinghouse, with miniature levers of the orthodox type, but with the lever interlocking all-electric, instead of through a purely mechanical system of tappets and cross-locks.

There were some diverting moments during our own installation of the work at Cardiff. The resident engineer was a man who had been literally born into signalling. His father, trained on the Great Western, had been Signal Engineer of one of the leading Indian railways, and his eldest son had his early training with Westinghouse. This son was a hard hitting character, and already had some tough experience in South America behind him when he took charge of the Cardiff job. Signalling to him was the very breath of life, and once on the job he did not tolerate interference gladly. One day they were fixing some concrete stools on which the ground shunt signals were to be mounted. One of the local signal inspectors came up and watched for a time. He was a rather humourless sanctimonious type and after a while said: 'I don't think that is very strong'. Like a flash came the reply: 'You try and push the b—— thing over!' Reproof for bad language came at once, but the complaint was passed upward through the hierarchy of the Signal Department until it reached headquarters, in Reading. I am afraid it was not taken very seriously there, and even more so when in some hilarity it was passed on to our Chief Constructional Engineer.

Another report, received just after the opening, at first puzzled those who had designed the signal operating circuits. It was that the lights in certain of the signals went out suddenly, and then a second or two later came on again, and remained normal thereafter. Enquiry revealed that the suspect units were mounted on lengthy gantries spanning many of the tracks. The steelwork had been fabricated by a sub-contractor in Scotland, but vertically above each of the running lines we had been required to fit smoke plates to prevent the direct upward exhaust from locomotives from impinging upon the cases containing the relay mechanism and the optical system. The smoke plates extended about 2ft outwards each side of the gantry structure. No locomotive enthusiast of today, least of all those belonging to the preservation groups or operating companies with Great Western motive power, needs to be reminded of the sharpness of the blast of Swindon locomotives when starting away; at Cardiff, in the 1930s there were not only the London expresses but very heavy freights which had been stopped on the centre roads. When such a blast hit one of those smoke plates near the outer end the force was sufficient to twist the lattice structure of the gantries, and the beam of light from the signal, accurately focused, was momentarily tilted upwards, and gave the impression that the light had gone out! We had to strengthen those gantries against twist.

The war years brought some unusual tasks to Westinghouse from the Great Western. The first came early in 1940 with the signalling for the new junction being laid in at Reading to connect with the Southern line. The existing connection, which diverged from the main lines immediately abreast of the East Main signalbox, could not be reached by trains passing through the station on the up relief or the goods lines, and for wartime purposes direct access was essential. The new junction was put in some distance east of the existing one in great urgency, with the signals and points worked electrically from a small power frame installed in the large East Main box. The time was not one to insist on standard GWR fittings. We had not supplied mechanical signal equipment to the company, and they told us to use the nearest we had. I remember going through endless old drawings, and then the question came up of seeing if we still had the patterns. There was no time to make new patterns in those hectic days. The biggest structure was a triple bracket signal, with its post between the up main and the down relief lines, and it was the most un-Great Western signal that was ever created. Its landing was supported on two massive baulks of timber; I can't remember the origin of the patterns I found for the spandrel brackets, and the pinnacles on the three-doll posts were ex-Great Central! There were five semaphore arms in all, and two shunt arms.

Then as the war situation changed and it was necessary to provide improved facilities for the flow of freight traffic to the south coast, examination of lines like the North to West, via Shrewsbury and Hereford, the old South Wales main, via Gloucester, and others showed that they were inadequately furnished with siding and freight loop accommodation. The loops had to be lengthened, dead-end sidings converted into long running loops, and in all cases the facing points at the entering ends of the loops were too far away from the existing signal boxes for manual operation. Fortunately we had, in Westinghouse, much experience of dealing with such problems by providing power for operating the remote functions by hand generator. There was more time to design the structures for the many stations at which these longer loops were put in, and we followed the later Great Western design using tubular posts for the main masts and also for the dolls. The only alien feature was the pinnacle or finial we used. The Great Central type we used at Reading new junction was for a wooden post, and the only pattern we had suitable for a tubular doll was a tall and elegant thing of purely American design. When some of my railway enthusiast friends got out and about again after the war, and saw those pinnacles, more than one asked me if they were to be the new post-war Great Western type, but I had to come clean and tell the truth how they originated.

Before leaving the wartime era I must refer to the distinguished engineer who succeeded C. M. Jacobs as Signal & Telegraph Engineer in February 1936, and who carried the department through the anxious years that followed. F. H. D. Page was a kindly man who I came to meet on a number of occasions just after the war. I shall always remember a conversation with him at Reading signal works in which he extolled the merits of expertly forged, hand-made point fittings compared to those produced by production-line methods, and how he deplored the growing situation that economic conditions no longer made such old-style fittings possible. He played as hard as he worked, and each year brought a cricket eleven and many camp followers to play Westinghouse, at Chippenham. It was always a keenly fought occasion, accompanied by many hilarious asides off the field. Page lived to a great age, and died in 1983, in his 101st year.

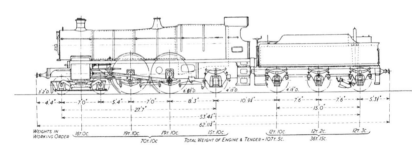

CHURCHWARD 4-4-2 (engines 171, 172, 179–190) NON-SUPERHEATED

Boiler :

Maximum diameter of barrel outside 5 ft. 6 in.
Tubes, small :
  Number 250
  Outside diameter ... ... 2 in.
  Length between tubeplates ... 15 ft. 2¾ in.

Heating Surfaces :
  Small tubes ... ... 1988·65 sq. ft.
  Firebox ... ... 154·26 sq. ft.
  Total ... ... 2142·91 sq. ft.

Grate Area ... ... 27·07 sq. ft.

Cylinders : Two
  Diameter ... ... 18 in.
  Stroke ... ... 30 in.

Motion : Type ... ... Stephenson
  Diameter of piston valves ... ... 10 in.
  Maximum travel of valves ... 6¼ in.
  Steam lap ... ... 1⅝ in.
  Exhaust clearance ... ... NIL
  Lead in full fore gear ... -0·15 in.
  Cut-off in full gear ... ... 77·5%

Tractive effort at 85% Working
  pressure ... ... 23,090 lb.

Factor of Adhesion :

$$\frac{\text{Adhesion weight}}{\text{Tractive effort}} = 3.78$$

6
Swindon: The Churchward Era

In this restless age, with all its changes in the sense of values, it is
becoming increasingly difficult to recall the aura of solid stability
and age-old railway tradition that was embodied in the single word,
Swindon, a works that knew only five bosses in the first 100 years of
its existence. But the Swindon which connoisseurs of locomotive
engineering history hold in such esteem is in reality no more than a
vast upstart growth of the 19th century compared to the ancient
town a mile to the south of the Junction, on the hilltop where
traditional highways from Devizes, Marlborough, Oxford and
Malmesbury meet, and where there has been a settlement from
Roman times. Although few of the artisans and their immediate
supervisors and foremen who made up the original work-force
'inside', as the local expression goes for men employed in the works,
were Wiltshiremen, there is no doubt that the placidity of the
surrounding countryside, and the incidence of country pastimes and
sport infused a spirit of West Country calm and contentment to
back up a great engineering evolution. On a smaller scale I became
conscious of the same atmosphere in the Saxby & Farmer
establishment when I joined Westinghouse at Chippenham.

Of course the rapid 19th century development of the Great
Western locomotive and carriage works, and the large housing
estates that grew up in the vicinity, known at first as New Swindon,
tended to outbalance older interests, population wise if nothing
else, and when the towns of Old and New Swindon were
incorporated in 1900 it was significant that a Great Western man,
no less than George Jackson Churchward, was unanimously elected
as the first Mayor of the Borough. Quite apart from the towering
status he subsequently attained as an engineer Churchward was an
embodiment of all that was best in a senior officer of the Great
Western Railway. He was a countryman by birth, and a lover and
crack exponent of country pursuits, having been born in the

charming village of Stoke Gabriel, overlooking the River Dart in South Devon. His ancestors had been yeomen in the district for centuries and his uncle was Lord of the Manor. Some years ago, in pursuance of another literary commission I visited Stoke Gabriel, and found many records of Churchwards in the parish records.

In the little church there is a stained glass window with the following inscription: 'To the Glory of God and in pious memory of the family of Churchward since 1485 of Hill in this parish. This window is erected by Frederick Churchward of Hill, September 29th 1906.' There also I discovered the family motto: *Ales Volat Propitiis*, of which a free translation is: 'May the flight of the birds be propitious'. I wonder how often G. J. Churchward recalled that family motto when his engines were making new British speed records! He was born in 1857, and but for the intransigence of certain landlords the broad gauge Dartmouth & Torbay Railway, connecting with the South Devon Railway at Torre, would have crossed the Dart within sight of his birthplace at Greenway Ferry and continued into Dartmouth itself. At a very early age it is evident that railways fired his imagination and at the age of 16 he entered the works of the South Devon railway at Newton Abbot as an articled pupil to John Wright, then Locomotive Superintendent of both the South Devon and the Cornwall Railways. In 1876 when both these railways had been absorbed by the Great Western, and he himself was still no more than 19 years of age, he was transferred to Swindon, to begin what proved to be his entire life's work.

The Locomotive, Carriage and Wagon Superintendent of the Great Western Railway, as his very title implied, had responsibility for a wide variety of work. It did not rest with the design, manufacture and maintenance of the rolling stock; he was responsible for locomotive running, and included on his pay-roll every driver, fireman, cleaner and shed labourer from end to end of the line. It could therefore be implied that any aspirant to the office would be a man of the widest interests and capabilities, recalling also that there was a second main works at Wolverhampton, where general overhaul was undertaken of many types of locomotive, while repair work of an intermediate nature was also undertaken at Newton Abbot. There was also an activity generally grouped as 'outside machinery', which included among other things the gigantic pumping installation involved in keeping the Severn Tunnel free of flooding.

When Churchward came to Swindon in 1876 he began a career of varied experience. For a man whose subsequent work was to have so wide and profound an influence on British locomotive design generally his stay in the Swindon drawing office was remarkably brief, and much of that time was spent in assisting Joseph Armstrong's third son, Joseph – 'Young Joe'. Joseph the elder was still in office when Churchward was transferred from Newton Abbot to Swindon, but he died in the following year at the relatively early age of 61.

When he succeeded to the office of Locomotive, Carriage and Wagon Superintendent William Dean put Young Joe on to the job of improving the Sanders and Bolitho form of the automatic vacuum brake, and after a spell on more general drawing office duties, which for a young man of 19 it can be imagined would not be very demanding, Churchward was assigned to help Young Joe. It was then that Churchward became very impressed with his ingenuity, but not with his business acumen. Eventually the Great Western had by far the best form of the vacuum automatic brake; but how much of it was directly due to Joseph Armstrong's work cannot now be traced, because he was completely careless when it came to patenting the many original ideas that were generally believed to be his, for he did not bother to do so. How he was killed on the line near Wolverhampton, taking a short cut home from a New Year's Eve party in 1888, is a sad story. His nephew, R. J. Armstrong, recalled a conversation he once had with Churchward many years afterwards when he was a draughtsman, and was summoned to the official residence. While they waited for the visitor who RJ was to conduct round the works, Churchward fell to reminiscing, and said: 'If your Uncle Joe had lived, I should not be occupying this house today as Locomotive Superintendent: he was a far cleverer man than I.'

While that may have been true in a strictly technical sense one is inclined to question whether the Great Western would have flourished as it did, in an age when free and easy ways, and a rather carefree outlook might not have countered the increasing stresses of 20th Century conditions. After the completion of the vacuum brake job both Joe Armstrong and Churchward were moved from the locomotive drawing office at Swindon. Both had evidently caught the eye of William Dean, and to broaden their experience Young Joe was appointed assistant to the Divisional Locomotive Running Superintendent, Swindon, and Churchward, Inspector of

Materials. In 1881, when he was still only 24 years of age Churchward was moved on to the Carriage and Wagon side as assistant to James Holden, who was then carriage Works Manager. He rose in stature so rapidly that only four years later when Holden left, to become Locomotive Superintendent of the Great Eastern Railway at Stratford, Churchward was promoted to take his place; in that same year his associate and close friend Joe Armstrong was transferred from Swindon to Wolverhampton, to become Assistant Divisional Superintendent and Works Manager at Stafford Road Works. This was generally regarded as a key appointment, and while serving there under his formidable uncle, George Armstrong, he was becoming regarded as the likely man to succeed William Dean as Chief when the time came. Joe Armstrong was then 29, and like Churchward a batchelor.

It is remarkable to recall that when Churchward received his first major appointment, in 1885, as Carriage Works Manager at Swindon, Sir Daniel Gooch was still Chairman of the Company, and remained so until his death in 1889. After Joe Armstrong's death in 1888 there seems to have been something of a hiatus in the continuity of promotion in the Locomotive Department, and it was not until 1896 that Dean brought Churchward from the Carriage to the Locomotive Works, to be Manager, and later also to be his chief assistant; and it can be noted in passing that it was not until he was 39 years of age that the future chief became directly, and exclusively, involved with locomotives, and then, officially at any rate, only with construction and repair – not design. It will perhaps come as a surprise and shock to some dedicated Great Western supporters when I suggest that Churchward was never an engine designer, as such, but that his genius lay in knowing a good thing when he saw it, and in co-ordinating the work of a team of designers who were each specialists in their own field. One could not pick out any feature of the designs that came so to distinguish Great Western practice in later years and say that it was pure Churchward; and yet he followed every line of development with the closest attention, spending hours on the drawing boards of the senior men most closely involved.

That attention began in earnest when he was appointed Locomotive Works Manager, and he became intimately involved not only with construction but with maintenance problems. He cast his net of investigation wide, studying current American and French practice, but while so doing he remained essentially an

English country gentleman, enjoying country sports, delighting in flower and vegetable growing, and dressing to look, for all the world, like the squire of the most rural of parishes. After the death of Young Joe Armstrong it began to be fairly clear that eventually Churchward was the man to succeed Dean, and to him personally the probability that the rest of his life's work would be in Swindon. While he himself once said: 'When other railways wanted a good man they looked to the Great Western', with the prospect of the Locomotive, Carriage and Wagon Superintendent's job in sight there was nothing elsewhere likely to tempt him away, and he was becoming more and more involved in the civic life of Swindon. I have mentioned earlier how, on the incorporation of Old and New Swindon he became the first Mayor of the Borough. I remember commenting upon the association of senior officers of the Locomotive Department with civic affairs to F. W. Hawksworth on one of my many talks with him, and he just tossed it on one side saying: 'Oh, it just went with the job!'

Churchward was certainly a railwayman to his fingertips, but that did not prevent him from being a considerable road user. His country pursuits took him to many places where there were no railways, and even before he came to Swindon in 1876 he had a car – steam driven, mostly home made, and fitted with a Merryweather boiler, as used on some contemporary fire engines. The story goes that he had his first petrol driven car in 1900, but of what make I do not know. It was built largely to his specification, and just as in later years he set much store on economic fuel consumption of his steam locomotives so he emphatically laid down certain parameters for the petrol consumption of that car. It was made in London, and the chauffeur who drove it down to Swindon was not likely to forget the acceptance trials for many a long day afterwards. The car was duly topped up with petrol, but the going was harder than anticipated, and six miles short of journey's end the supply was exhausted. There were no such things as village filling stations in those days, and the unfortunate driver had to hire a pony and trap, drive into Swindon, get some more petrol and go back to top up the tank. That however was nothing to what faced him the following day, when Churchward went with him for a hill-climbing test.

They took the Marlborough road out of Swindon, and ran pleasantly along beside the single-track line of the Midland & South Western Junction Railway until coming to the village of Ogbourne St George, where Churchward stopped him, and directed him on to the road that leads over the downs to Aldbourne. The escarpment ahead of them looked formidable, and the one-inch Ordnance Survey map shows it crowned by tumuli, ancient British settlements, and the accompaniments of wild remote hill country. The London born chauffeur was aghast. 'Yes', said Churchward; 'That's the hill the car's got to climb.' On the worst pitch the road ascends 200ft in little more than $\frac{1}{4}$ mile, about 1 in 7. 'Call that an 'ill?', the poor chap exclaimed; 'You calls that an 'ill! I calls it a b—— mountain!' Despite such protests the car climbed the hill satisfactorily and Churchward accepted delivery.

Sports and pastimes apart, by 1900 he was involved in one of the most critical phases of his career. His chief, William Dean, had done a magnificent job since he was called upon to succeed Joseph Armstrong in 1877, but before even the end of the century his memory was failing and the directors found they could no longer transact business with him. He, like James Inglis, the Engineer-in-chief, reported direct to the Board, and not through the General Manager. The Chairman, then Viscount Emlyn, realising what kind of man Churchward was, and having already decided upon the eventual succession, determined upon one of the kindest courses of action that could be imagined. They knew that Dean had come to place the utmost reliance on Churchward, and that despite his increasing disabilities in other directions this relationship showed no sign of diminishing. So, while Churchward was authorised to go ahead with his developments in boiler design, high raised Belpaire fireboxes, and the elimination of steam domes, Dean was encouraged to believe that all these were his own highly commendable ideas. The directors did not forget the inestimable services he had rendered in the past, particularly in the many difficult problems that had been involved at the time of the final abolition of the broad gauge. In addition to the Chairman the two directors principally involved were Alexander Hubbard and Walter Robinson. All three had engines named after them. There was a Dean 4–2–2 named *Emlyn*, built in 1898, while another of the same class built three years earlier and originally named *Tartar*, after one of the broad gauge eight footers was renamed *Walter Robinson*. The name *Alexander Hubbard* was put on to one of the new 4–4–0s of the Badminton class, built in 1898.

Churchward's interest in American locomotive practice is generally considered to have developed from his friendship with A. W. Gibbs of the Pennsylvania Railroad. In the 1890s, when the

4–4–0, the 'American', as it was known in the USA, was still the most popular general service locomotive in North America, and with the great majority having the conventional Stephenson link motion inside the frames, there was a world of difference between the gaunt, highly functional machines that ran many of the crack trains of the USA, and in other areas the freights too, and the neat, handsomely proportioned British 4–4–0s on which everything remotely resembling machinery was tucked inside, out of sight. The Great Western Badmintons with their outside frames, and outside-framed bogies were typical of the era, no less in their gorgeous colouring. One fundamental difference lay in the use of bar instead of plate frames, and the former made possible a highly advantageous design at the front end. But Churchward out of his kindness of heart towards Dean's susceptibilities seems to have progressed warily. The Badminton class was the first in which his new precepts were at all embodied, and then only in the high raised Belpaire firebox and the extended smokebox. But for these subtle changes they looked like a Dean design, except that one of them, the *Waterford*, was given a domeless boiler.

The Badmintons did excellent work, particularly on routes like that from Bristol to Shrewsbury via the Severn Tunnel, where single-wheelers were virtually precluded because of the long and heavy gradients, and the performance of *Waterford* gave Churchward the answer he needed so far as future boiler design was concerned. In 1900 he went more boldly into the unorthodox, so far as Dean was concerned, with the Atbara class of 4–4–0s, with domeless parallel boilers, high raised Belpaire fireboxes, and with the flowing curves of the running plate above the outside frames replaced by a starkly functional straight frame. Yet the new engines, in all the literature and photographs that were published about them, were wholly attributed to Dean; and such was the kindly hand of Churchward behind the scenes at Swindon that Dean firmly believed he was entirely responsible for them, and worthy of the praise bestowed upon their work – if not their aesthetics. Then, when the time came for Churchward to put the fruits of his American contacts and close study into practice, in the building of the first Great Western express passenger 4–6–0, in 1902, he retained one predominant feature of British practice, the continuous inside plate frames on engine No 100.

In its issue of November 1902 *The Railway Magazine* had a beautiful lithographed colour plate of engine No 100; but it had no

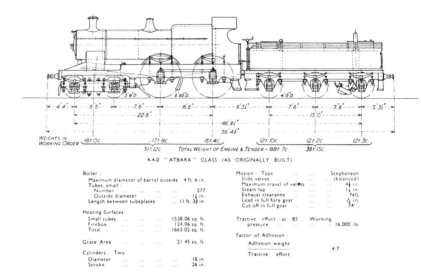

4-4-0 "ATBARA" CLASS (AS ORIGINALLY BUILT)

Boiler :					Motion : Type			Stephenson
Maximum diameter of barrel outside				4 ft. 6 in.	Slide valves			(balanced)
Tubes, small :					Maximum travel of valves	...		4¼ in.
Number	...	...	...	277	Steam lap	...		1¼ in.
Outside diameter		...		1¾ in.	Exhaust clearance	...		NIL
Length between tubeplates		...	11 ft. 3¼ in.	Lead in full fore gear	...		⅛ in.
					Cut-off in full gear	...	...	74".
Heating Surfaces :								
Small tubes	...	...	...	1538 06 sq. ft.	Tractive effort at 85 . Working			
Firebox	...	...	...	124 96 sq. ft.	pressure	...	...	16,000 lb.
Total	..	...	...	1663 02 sq. ft.				
					Factor of Adhesion :			
Grate Area	...	...	...	21 45 sq. ft.	Adhesion weight			
					———————			4 7
Cylinders : Two					Tractive effort			
Diameter	...	...	...	...	18 in.			
Stroke	...	...	...	...	26 in.			

sooner emerged from Swindon Works, in the previous March, than Charles Rous-Marten had delivered himself, at great length on the design of the engine, repeatedly attributing this or that feature entirely to Dean. Now from those who knew him best, and were in his confidence on many topics, one might have assumed that 'CR-M' had, as one of his friends put it, an almost 'indecent familiarity' with the inner workings of our great locomotive building establishments; and so far as Swindon was concerned would have been aware of the outward façade that was being maintained in respect of Dean's continued and complete involvement with every new feature of design in Great Western locomotives. Furthermore, there was not a whisper of his retirement, in June 1902. When he was persuaded to give up by the kindest of suggestion by the three directors with whom he was officially concerned, he slipped away almost unnoticed, to a quiet retreat that had been found for him at Folkestone; the first reference to his going made in *The Railway Magazine* was when F. G. Wright was elected Mayor of Swindon at the beginning of 1903. It was then noted that he was Assistant Locomotive, Carriage & Wagon Superintendent of the GWR, having been appointed to that office when Churchward had succeeded Dean in the previous June. Wright's election provided yet another instance of Hawksworth's assertion that civic honours at Swindon 'went with the job'.

With Churchward now officially in the saddle the great development that he had begun, almost surreptitiously, went rapidly ahead. The subsequent history, particulary as it concerned the express passenger locomotives has been very fully documented,* but as Swindon personnel were involved the development at first took two major lines, the boiler and the valve gear. In the paper he presented to the Institution of Mechanical Engineers in 1906, 'Large Locomotive Boilers', Churchward himself revealed how closely he had studied American practice, and how much he was beholden to the transactions of the Master Mechanics Association; but also evident was the extent to which his chief assistant F. G. Wright, and his Works Manager H. C. King were in his confidence. At that time the Swindon expert on valve gears was a leading draughtsman, W. H. Pearce, and it was he who designed the special setting of the Stephenson link motion, with long valve laps, and long travel, and also the celebrated arrangement for the 'scissors' form of the Walschaerts valve gear used on the four-cylinder 4–4–2 No 40 *North Star* which led to such an unholy row with R. M. Deeley, of the Midland Railway.

Churchward wanted to use Walschaerts radial valve gear on No 40, having been impressed by the working of the de Glehn compound Atlantics purchased from France, and anxious, on a high speed engine, to eliminate the vibration that was sometimes obtrusive when his two-cylinder engines with the Stephenson link motion were running fast, and pulled up to relatively short cut-offs. But Churchward would not have any valve gear outside, and in scheming out an arrangement Pearce hit upon the idea of eliminating eccentrics on the driving axle by using the crosshead of one cylinder to provide the equivalent of an eccentric on the other cylinder. In June 1905 Pearce made a wooden model of the proposed arrangement, and showed it to Churchward. The model related only to the gear for the two inside cylinders. The spindles for the outside cylinder valves were, it was intended, to be actuated by rocking shafts connected to the motion of the inside cylinders. Churchward was delighted with the idea, and gave instructions that it should be included on the prototype four-cylinder Atlantic on which the design work was then well advanced.

Meanwhile Deeley, when assistant to S. W. Johnson on the Midland, had a very similar idea, with the object of eliminating the

* *The GWR Stars, Castles and Kings*, published by David & Charles

eccentrics needed on the driving axle when Stephenson link motion was used. The story goes that Johnson turned it down flat, but when Deeley succeeded to the position of Locomotive Superintendent he had the scheme worked out in detail. The subsequent dates are important, recalling that at Swindon Pearce had his wooden model completed and showed it to Churchward in June 1905. Deeley's gear was intended for a two-cylinder engine, with inside cylinders, and he had more room to manoeuvre than Pearce; but on 11 August 1905 he applied for a patent for the arrangement, and this was granted in June 1906. Churchward's new four-cylinder Atlantic No 40 was completed at Swindon in April 1906, but when Deeley learned about the valve gear he was furious and wrote to the GWR, threatening all sorts of dire penalties for infringement of patent. But Churchward had no difficulty in proving that the Swindon form of the gear was designed and the wooden model made before even Deeley had lodged his patent application. As things turned out No 40 was the only Great Western engine to be fitted with the gear, while on the Midland only the ten 4–4–0s of the 999 class were so fitted.

Still on the subject of valve gears, just after the end of the second world war I had the pleasure of meeting J. C. Crebbin, the eminent miniature steam locomotive engineer. He was a man of considerable wealth, and had in earlier years been intimately acquainted with Churchward. He told me of an occasion when he went to Swindon in company with Sir Aubrey Brocklebank, a director who also became well known in miniature railway circles for his interest in the Ravenglass & Eskdale Railway. In conclave with Churchward the conversation ranged round varying points of locomotive design, and eventually centred upon the relative merits of the Stephenson link motion and of the Walschaerts gear. As they gathered round someone's drawing board and rival opinions were being voiced, Churchward listened carefully, and then he turned to Sir Aubrey and said: 'You're the first b—— director I've ever met who knew anything about valve gears!'

Churchward's 4–6–2 No 111 *The Great Bear* has always been something of an enigma to many Great Western enthusiasts, who have been intrigued to know why it was ever built. A most perceptive commentator, the late J. N. Maskelyne, refers to it at some length in the second volume of his book of immaculately executed drawings *Locomotives I have known*. He writes:

It occurred to one of the directors that if the GWR company was being supplied with the finest and most efficient engines in the country, what a splendid thing it would be if the GWR could claim it had the largest engine. It would act as a spur to the intensive advertising campaign that was being launched. And so the directors consulted Churchward, and he told them flatly that if they wanted such an engine they could have it; but it would cost a tidy sum and they would never be able to use it. Nevertheless the directors voted in favour of having Britain's largest locomotive, and Churchward was instructed to build it, as cheaply as possible.

Well that is one version. To me however it did not seem to ring quite true. Churchward always said that the boiler was the main consideration in locomotive design, and in his celebrated paper to the Institution of Mechanical Engineers 'Large Locomotive Boilers' he illustrated no fewer than nine built in the USA that were vastly bigger than anything then contemplated in Great Britain. Maskelyne emphasised the strength of the advertising campaign for the South Devon and Cornish holiday resorts, and already this would lead to the need for much heavier trains than hitherto in the height of the season; having the boiler particularly in mind one could quite understand Churchward wanting to try something far bigger than his standard No 1, as used on the Saints and Stars in readiness for future requirements. Whether the actual proposal came from Churchward himself or from a member of the Locomotive Committee of the Board is immaterial, but the fact remains that on 30 January 1907 the Board voted a sum of £4,400 for the construction of a Pacific. Subsequently an additional £860 was voted to cover further expenses. An interesting point is that at the time of that first authorisation only one Churchward four-cylinder engine was running, Atlantic No 40, *North Star*. The first of the Star class proper, No 4001 *Dog Star*, was not completed at Swindon until February 1907. Maskelyne suggests that Churchward had been in trouble with certain members of the Board before this, over the high cost of his new engines; but the row that led to comparison of building costs at Swindon with those at Crewe, and which led to the interchange trial of 1910, came much later.

In the course of some investigations at Swindon for my book *The GWR Stars, Castles and Kings*, and some visits I was privileged to pay to that 'holy of holies', the locomotive drawing office, I saw that the general arrangement drawing of *The Great Bear* bore the initials F.W.H., and my host on that day confirmed that Hawksworth himself had actually made that drawing. I had met him several times previously and always found him most friendly, and I decided then I must seek another interview with him, in his retirement. I little imagined how soon, and in what intimidating circumstances the chance to talk to him would come. I was invited to lecture to the Swindon Engineering Society one evening, and after dinner with some of the leading locomotive men of the Western Region we went on to the lecture hall to find a crowded audience with Hawksworth himself sitting in the front row! I cannot remember now what particular aspect of Great Western locomotive history my lecture covered; but as usual on such occasions, at question time the discussion ranged far and wide. Then one member of the audience, not, I afterwards discovered, a railwayman, asked about *The Great Bear*, and out of the corner of my eye I saw Hawksworth, who until then had been taking no more than a casual interest in the question and answer session, sit bolt upright. This was it. So, in some trepidation, I put forward my own belief that *The Great Bear* had been built primarily as an exercise in larger boiler design, to gain experience against the time when larger engines than the Stars would be necessary. When making my reply I glanced to where Hawksworth was sitting and saw that he had relaxed again and was smiling, and before concluding my remarks to this questioner I referred to Mr Hawksworth's presence at the meeting and his involvement with the design, and asked him, across the floor how far my suppositions were correct. He nodded approval, and we had a long talk about it after the meeting closed.

Churchward's predictions as to the usefulness of the engine, as referred to by Maskelyne proved true enough, because at that time the civil engineering department was very touchy about the weights its track would take, and the great length of the engine despite its carefully designed trailing radial truck did not take kindly to curves. There were reports of that truck derailing itself when setting back on to a train in No 1 platform at Paddington. Maskelyne, whose lifelong enthusiasm took him frequently to Paddington, said the engine was 'a holy terror for slipping'. This I could well believe, because Pacifics as a breed are not nearly so sure-footed as 4–6–0s. But comparing the weight distribution of *The Great Bear* with that of a Gresley A1 Pacific of 1923, while in both cases each coupled axle carried a weight of 20 tons, the Great Western engine had 17.4 tons on the radial trailing axle, whereas the Gresley engine had only 15.4 tons. When the fundamental weight transfer took place on starting away with a heavy load, the lighter axle loading on the trailing truck of the Gresley engine would enable it to 'sit back on its haunches' more readily, and avoid the weight transfer from the coupled axles.

I saw *The Great Bear* only once. After the first world war when the engine was normally confined to a single daily round trip from Paddington to Bristol and back, at most, there was still a tremendous amount of interest in the engine, and it was symbolised in January 1920, when *The Railway Magazine*, having commissioned the artist 'F. Moore' of the Locomotive Publishing Company to paint the picture, published a large colour plate showing the engine in its wartime plain green livery. Unfortunately the colour plate, though beautifully executed and reproduced, was so large that it had to be folded, and the creases have not improved its appearance in the ensuing 63 years! 'The Bear' used to work in a link of only four engines, one of which was the pioneer 5ft 8in 2–8–0 No 4700. One of its duties was the 10.45am down from Paddington, returning from Bristol on a train that used to be known as the 'Up Ilfracombe' – why, I have no idea. It was a heavy train and ran up non-stop from Bath, arriving at Paddington at 4.10pm. It was on this duty that I saw the great engine in 1923, on a day when, alas, I did not have my camera with me. In following the empty stock out of the arrival platform it was stopped briefly, and in beautiful sunshine it would have made the fine picture that I failed to secure.

There were many stories of 'The Bear'. A Bristol driver with whom I had several interesting footplate rides told me what a splendid steaming engine it was. He fired on it many times when it was working the heavy night express goods from Avonmouth to Paddington, having come down on the 6.30pm Plymouth express; nevertheless I have always felt the most telling commendation of the engine came from a young engineer who was assistant superintendent at Old Oak Common, in the 1920s. He was conducting a party of graduates from the Institution of Mechanical Engineers round the shed one Saturday afternoon in the early spring of 1925, when alas the engine had been converted into a 4–6–0, and fitted with a Castle boiler. The visit was nearly over and a little group of us collected round this young assistant in the cab of a Star class engine, while he gossiped pleasantly about Great Western engines in general. Inevitably the conversion of *The Great*

Bear came up, and it was soon evident that he regretted the change as much as any amateur enthusiast. It had been one of 'his' engines, at Old Oak Common, and he wound up the conversation saying: 'I *liked* the "Bear" '. One could not say more than that, and with the 'scrapping' of the engine it could well be said that the Churchward era ended.

7
GWR and the Press: J. A. Kay

The GWR never had a greater friend than John Aiton Kay, Editor of *The Railway Gazette* from 1905 until his death in 1949. The greatest and most securely established of businesses cannot entirely disregard the field of public relations, and the activities of what is now called the media in its great diversity of forms; but at the turn of the century its power and ultimate influence seems to have been not even vaguely envisaged or comprehended by some of the greatest English railway managers. The ground had been broken, if no more than slightly, by the founding of *The Railway Magazine* in July 1897, originally independent, but absorbed into the publishing empire Transport (1910) Ltd over which John Kay reigned as Managing Director for so many years. G. A. Sekon, the founder and first editor of *The Railway Magazine* has told how he went 'cap in hand' to Paddington seeking an interview with the General Manager, J. L., afterwards Sir Joseph Wilkinson, for the first of what became a notable series of 'Illustrated Interviews' with famous railway personalities; but from what Sekon wrote some 50 years later that 'interview' was not so relaxed and friendly as one might have imagined from reading it in print.

Wilkinson took a lot of persuasion that information other than purely business and financial matters would be of any interest, and Sekon was required to submit in writing a list of the questions he wished to ask, to which written replies were given. It was all woven, with no little journalistic skill, into a most entertaining article that gave the impression of complete spontaneity, and Wilkinson himself was so pleased that in the December 1897 issue he contributed an article himself which showed that, among other things, he had a rare sense of humour. It was only a short piece, entitled 'The General Manager', and apart from a very revealing organisational tree of his department, and an extraordinary full page picture of the interior of Paddington station, it was a remarkably light-hearted essay at a time when any injection of humour into railway literature was apt to be of the elephantine kind. But that picture of Paddington is indeed a curiosity. It was taken looking outwards from above platforms 4 and 5. There are short strings of covered vans in 2 and 4, an engine standing far ahead in No 1, and a very ornate clerestory-roofed saloon at the buffer stops in No 5. Otherwise, the station is completely deserted. It seems a strange choice to represent so usually busy a *passenger* station and one is inclined to wonder if it is not a leg-pull on Wilkinson's part!

In *The Railway Gazette* Kay directed his attention to the professional aspects of railways, management, engineering and operation, and by 1918 he had gathered in all the rivals: *The Railway Times*, in 1914, and *The Railway News* in 1918. Furthermore *The Railway Engineer* had come under his management in 1919, though it was not physically incorporated into *The Railway Gazette* until 1935. But by these amalgamations Kay had in many ways become the spokesman of the railway companies – a friend of all, or nearly all. There was one occasion when he badly upset an eminent general manager, none other than Sir Guy Granet of the Midland, in suggesting that there was a long anticipated facility that could be looked forward to under his management. Granet was so furious that he cancelled all Midland Railway advertising in *The Railway Gazette*! It was far different with the Great Western, and while in reporting activities of all the railways, overseas as well as home, he was always strictly impartial I learned later that he had a specially warm regard for the Great Western, as its top management and officers had for him.

I first became aware of him, as a mighty power behind the scenes, in the late autumn of 1919, as a regular reader of *The Railway Magazine*. That year, as from midnight on Friday 26 September, there was a general strike of railwaymen, a date that I remember all the more vividly because it was the last day of the school summer holidays, and had the strike begun only a few hours earlier I, and many others, would not have been able to travel from home to boarding school. There were many regrets at the timing of the strike among our school community! In the November issue of *The Railway Magazine* I read of the experiences of the technical editor of John Kay's railway journals, Charles S. Lake, as a volunteer engineman; but what interested me as much at the time, and still more so in more recent years was the manner in which Lake was recruited and enrolled for the service. Although living as far afield, for those days, as Bedford and commuting daily, he was a full-time member of the Transport (1910) group of journals. He managed to get enough petrol to drive his car up to London on the first Monday of the strike, to report to the office; but on arrival Kay sent for him and said that the GWR had been in touch, and asked if any of the staff would be prepared to act as volunteers. Would he like to have a go, as an engineman, for Lake was practically trained and a fully qualified locomotive engineer. The point to notice at once is that although he lived at Bedford, here was Kay offering his services to the Great Western!

After that things moved fast. Kay took him straight away to Paddington, and introduced him to R. H. Nicholls, Superintendent of the Line, and to C. Crump, the London Divisional Locomotive Superintendent, with the result that he was instructed to book on at 11am next morning as a fireman. Lake was no youngster even then, having been born as long previously as 1872; but he was a fit man, and the tasks involved in the strike service, though needing experience, were not unduly strenuous. From the outset the GWR began operating services between Paddington and Slough, and Paddington and Reading, and, for the former, engines of the standard Churchward 2–6–0 type were used, working tender first on the homeward journey, with stops at all stations in both directions. Kay was nothing if not a publicist, and on the first day that his staff man, Lake, was to fire the 2.45pm from Paddington he, by arrangement with his GWR friends in the top circles, arrived with a staff photographer from Topical Press, and a number of pictures were taken of Lake and his driver preparing the engine, No 5350, for the run, one of which included Kay himself, immaculate in bowler hat, rolled umbrella, and the bow-tie that he wore on every conceivable occasion, standing alongside the engine, with the Chief Locomotive Foreman at Paddington. The article that Lake subsequently wrote for *The Railway Magazine* was deeply interesting on its own account, but it was doubly so through Kay's enterprise in getting so many very Topical photographs to go with it.

At that time, of course, Kay was a mere name to me, and it was not until many years later when I had met him personally that I recognised him as the bowler hatted gentleman in that strike-time picture at Paddington. In my student days at Imperial College J. F. Gairns was Editor of *The Railway Magazine*. He had taken over from the founder G. A. Sekon, in 1910, and had remained in the chair through several changes in ownership. He was later Chief Assistant Editor of *The Railway Gazette*. My great friend Macgregor Pearson, was for a time Hon Secretary of the Engineering Society of the College, and as a great railway enthusiast persuaded Gairns to come and address one of our meetings on locomotive development. He was disappointingly pedestrian in his approach and style, and his lecture left nothing but poor impressions upon a crowd of eager, high spirited students. One of my friends who later earned no small distinction as an aircraft designer said afterwards that he wanted to rag him, but altogether the audience was discreetly polite, however unimpressed they were. He was a kindly and pleasant man to talk to, but his rather dogged and plodding nature was to some extent reflected in the editorial quality of *The Railway Magazine* in the 1920s. He died in 1930 at the early age of 54, and it was then that a considerable change came over the railway literary world.

Up to that time there were rarely any mentions of occasions when things had gone wrong other, of course, than accidents in which there were injuries to passengers and loss of life; but on the Great Western particularly when traffic conditions got positively chaotic I remember so well the lead-up to one August holiday when I was staying with my parents at Paignton, and my sister was travelling down from London to join us for the last week in July. I cannot now remember quite how I managed to brief her in advance, but the fact remains that on arrival she presented me with a remarkably complete log of the journey, full details of which I still have. But what a journey it was! On Saturdays the first part of the Torbay Limited was booked to run non-stop to Paignton, and with no more than eight coaches and Star class 4–6–0, *Queen Matilda* in spanking condition, the job should have been easy enough. Despite one or two checks the train was speeding over the Langport cut-off line in good time to pass Taunton three or four minutes early, but once into the stream of traffic from the north things rapidly worsened, and it eventually took that supposedly crack train 33 minutes to cover the last $2\frac{1}{4}$ miles from Torquay to Paignton!

Of course we had been on the station ready for the hopefully punctual arrival of the train and I could see enough and more of the utter confusion and congestion that reigned in the 53 minutes we had waited, in the last 20 of which *Queen Matilda* and its train had waited patiently at the home signal just outside. Many trains terminated at Paignton. There were no carriage sidings at Goodrington then, and empty stock had to be drawn back to Newton Abbot. Moreover 4–6–0 engines were not permitted south of Paignton, so that trains for Kingswear had to change engines in a cramped and inadequate layout, with single line working immediately beyond; and when all trains were running out of course the delays just piled up. The same thing happened every Saturday during the summer, but everyone concerned seemed to take it as a matter of course, and the only reference I can recall to exceptional Saturday traffic to the West of England is a press photograph taken at Paddington just before the August Bank Holiday week-end showing engines for *five* sections of the Cornish Riviera Express coupled together and backing down towards the station. That was in 1926, and we can well wonder how those trains fared further down the line!

The change in editorial staff on the Tothill Street group of railway journals took place just about the time I was submitting my own first essays, and it was not long before I was invited to meet W. A. Willox, who had been appointed to succeed Gairns, as Editor of *The Railway Magazine*, and Associate Editor of *The Railway Gazette*. Willox was a railway civil engineer, previously a Divisional Engineer on the Southern, and a son of William Willox who had been Chief Engineer of the Metropolitan. Willox was a man of vastly different temperament from Gairns. There were many times when he would dearly have liked to call a spade a b—— shovel, but had to restrain his pen in deference to the conciliatory attitude John Kay always displayed towards any failings that were revealed. This was particularly the case when dealing with the Great Western.

The centenary of the company, in the early Autumn of 1935, was celebrated in appropriately magnificent style, by a lunch on the actual centenary day at Bristol, and a great banquet at Grosvenor House on 30 October, at which HRH The Prince of Wales was the principal guest. But when Christmas came, dense fog and severe frost reduced the passenger service to something near chaos in many large centres, but particularly at Paddington. It had always been a major point in the operating philosophy of the Great Western Railway, that the man on the spot should be left to get on with the job, without the need of centralised direction. Platform inspectors, signalmen, locomotive foremen, were regarded as responsible men in whose hands the day-to-day running of the trains could be left;

but just before Christmas 1935 the clerk of the weather descended on the GWR, and to a lesser extent on other railways running into London, with extreme severity. The company had not yet begun to use the public address system in dealing with crowds, and the morning was not far advanced at Paddington before it seemed that no one had the slightest idea of what was happening. Platform inspectors were as bewildered as any of the thousands of passengers who were hoping to get away from London for Christmas. The following story was told to me by a railwayman from another company – a reliable witness – who had reserved seats on the 11.10am express (2hr to Birmingham) for Shrewsbury.

A string of coaches, without roof boards, was drawn into one of the middle departure platforms about 11.15, and the waiting crowd of passengers surged upon it, some finding seats with numbers corresponding to their reservation tickets, but most, realising the confusion, just got in where they could. This 'kerfuffle' was just subsiding when a portentously grave looking platform inspector came walking down the platform shouting 'First stop Truro: first stop Truro'!! The response to this announcement can well be imagined, but it then appeared that the only people on the train who were not startled out of their wits were the dining car crew, who firmly believed they were on a relief train for Penzance, and were most disinclined to move. My friend and his family who had found their 'reserved seats' in a coach near to the front of the train were now all agog; he got out on the platform, when out of the dense freezing fog he saw an engine backing down. With his railway instincts now well and truly aroused he suggested to the bewildered platform inspector that it might be a good idea to ask the driver what train he thought he was coupling on to. In a deceptively high sing-song voice that worthy replied: 'I'm going home'. It was my friend who then chipped in, with: 'Where the hell's that?' 'Landore top link man', came the smiling reply. The consummation of this unholy muddle was now complete. Paddington had the stock and the dining car crew of a Cornish relief, the passengers for the 11.10am to Birkenhead, and the engine for the 11.55am to Swansea and West Wales all in one!

This was only one case, and happening as early in the day as 11.30am one can well imagine how things became later. Immediately after the holiday the national press was deluged with letters of complaint, some of them ill-informed, all of them scathing, and while hitting at the railways generally the Great

Western came in for a major share of the criticism, particularly in respect of the events of Christmas Eve at Paddington. The situation was serious enough for high authority to appeal to John Kay to publish some sort of explanation that would offer reasons why such conditions had developed. I saw Willox a few days afterwards, and he was still seething with indignation. Kay had apparently instructed him to write what amounted to an apologia for the Great Western, based on a sheaf of reports he had received from Paddington. Orders being orders he had drafted an extremely kind leading article, but his sentiments were far otherwise. 'Apologia', he exclaimed to me, 'I'd have sacked the General Manager!'

This is what he wrote, and duly received Kay's blessing:

Christmas Traffic Delays

So long as there are intermittent traffic peaks far beyond the day-to-day normal, it is inevitable that some inconvenience must be suffered by the travelling public at such periods. The traffics that had to be carried by the railways this Christmas were heavier than ever, and the conditions of railway operation were, particularly in some areas, almost unprecedently difficult. Fog, frost and bitter cold played their part in diverting much unexpected traffic from road to rail; in necessitating slow running with consequent delays to trains; in freezing pipes and signals, and in coating the ground with ice, so making the lot of the railwaymen unusually hard and hazardous, not only in preparing trains for their passengers but also in almost every phase of their duties; and in taking an unusually heavy toll of the staff in illness. In all these circumstances it is perhaps less extraordinary that there were heavy delays on some lines than that on others the delays were comparatively light, and that those who suffered inconvenience at least suffered it in safety. While the problem of peak traffic remains, it can be eased mainly by the encouragement of every member of the railway staffs to do his best and to use his initiative to the utmost, but not of course without discretion. There is certainly room for improvement here; instances have been reported to us of railwaymen shirking responsibilities the shouldering of which might have eased the lot of whole trainloads of passengers. On the other hand we have learnt with pleasure of many instances of resources and enterprise, the results of which were very appreciably to ease the traffic situation. The men who thus responsibly exercised initiative deserve well, and, although they cannot be specified and may not be directly rewarded they have the satisfaction that comes of tasks well done.

So much by way of a general introduction; then on particularly to the Great Western. The leading article continued:

> Devotion to duty also characterised the staff of the Great Western Railway, which suffered such serious disorganisation on the days immediately preceding Christmas that it has been the subject of correspondence in the press. A most unfortunate combination of circumstances was responsible for these conditions. Apart from the widespread and at times extremely dense fog, and the bitter cold, together imposing those obstacles to which we have already referred there were two circumstances unprecedented and unlikely to recur which contributed towards the breakdown. Owing to a threat of a coal strike, abnormal movements of coal from South Wales had to be handled just before Christmas; the coal trains not merely occupied running lines and by the weather conditions aforementioned became subject to heavy delays, but – because of the general increase in passenger traffic – they could not all be disposed of, and many sidings normally required for stabling coaching stock were occupied by the coal wagons. The other contribution to the trouble was the fact that the main London carriage depot at Old Oak Common is in process of enlargement, and during its present transition stage, some of the accommodation is necessarily in the hands of the contractors. While these circumstances cannot be expected to mollify a travelling public that suffered discomfort and inconvenience at a time when it had hoped for happiness and general good will, yet we feel they ought to be placed on record. It may be assumed that the experience of the Great Western at Christmas has brought home to the management the possibility of undertaking certain measures to deal with future emergencies. The loud speaker, for example, was used to very good effect in directing the crowds at certain other London stations. All progress is the result of trial and error, and a repetition of such unusual disorganisation as travellers suffered need not be feared.

My own experience of very severe delay in South Devon in the summer of 1925, and which recurred for several summers afterwards was completely cured, first by building extensive carriage sidings at Goodrington Sands, just to the south of Paignton, which obviated the necessity of moving trains of empty stock back to Newton Abbot, and by the installation of a turntable at Kingswear large enough to take even the King class engines. There was thereafter no need for through trains to change their 4–6–0 engines for a 2–6–2 tank before proceeding beyond Paignton. When holidays with pay increased the summer week-end traffic to unprecedented heights after the second world war, while petrol rationing prevailed, the facilities that had been installed in South Devon in the 1930s proved adequate, but there were still delays as trains bunched west of Taunton.

In 1944 when the war was nearing its climax with preparations for re-entry to mainland Europe in readiness for 'the longest day' and the great assault upon the Normandy beaches, the Ministry of War Transport gave the strictest instructions to the four main line railways of Great Britain that on no account were any extra passenger trains to be run, and indeed no extra coaches were to be added to the normal rakes of the regularly scheduled trains. It was fully expected that once the invasion was launched heavy retaliatory air attacks would be made on our lines of communication to the South Coast ports, and that extra passenger trains, or heavier regular trains could be an additional embarrassment. What was not expected, by the great bulk of the population at any rate, was that the enemy would begin the flying bomb (V1) attacks at this very time. While the V1 was a very inaccurate weapon in itself the very uncertainty of where each one was going to fall kept the whole London area on tenterhooks with apprehension; and when it was learned that the rest of the country was largely immune it was no more than natural that everyone who could get away to the country or to the sea for a few days' respite sought to do so. And people of every estate flocked to Paddington, to find, of course, that there was no room in the trains, and that no extras could be run. Although the attack began during the night of 15–16 June, with flying bombs then launched against the Greater London area at a rate of about 1000 a week, a high proportion of them had failed to arrive. Even so the number of people actually killed was also running at around 1000 a week.

The natural desire to get away reached crisis point on Saturday morning 29 July. The appalling crowding of the regular trains had been witnessed with the deepest concern by all those responsible for train working on the Great Western, and what happened on that Saturday morning did not take anyone by surprise. Unlike more normal times of extreme pressure this was no time for leaving things to the man on the ground. All the senior traffic officers were at Paddington, with the General Manager himself, Sir James Milne, very much in command. What happened that morning came to me later from two unimpeachable sources, Major J. Dewar, Publicity Officer of the GWR, who could have regaled the national press with the railway crowd story of the century, had he been permitted, and John Kay. One remained completely silent; the other published so heavily censored an editorial note that anyone not actually in London at the time would have had any idea how terribly serious the situation became. From an early hour the crowds surged into Paddington until The Lawn and the platforms were one solid mass of humanity, and for the first time in its history the station was closed.

The scheduled trains, with their un-strengthened formations were totally inadequate to get the people away. More and more arrived, and lengthy queues controlled by mounted police formed up on the pavements of Eastbourne Terrace. An appeal was made by telephone to the Ministry of War Transport to relax, even for one day, the ban on more trains – No! Still the queues lengthened. Flying bombs were heard detonating in the distance, and those looking out on the densely packed multitude on The Lawn wondered what would happen if one landed in their midst. Another appeal by phone to the Ministry – No!! Eventually Sir James Milne could stand it no longer, and he personally rang the Minister, and said that his car was waiting, and if he did not get a satisfactory answer *at once* he was going straight to Downing Street. In a very short time someone very high up in the Ministry was sent to see for himself. Meanwhile the Great Western had also appealed to London Transport, which had immediately responded by suspending all Underground bookings to any of the Paddington stations. Once the man from the Ministry had arrived and seen the appalling risks of having such a vast number of people in so confined an area permission was given readily enough to run more trains. He did not say how many, neither did he wait to see how it was done. He did not know what the Great Western could do in an emergency.

There was no more waiting. Down at Old Oak Common a dozen or more trains were already marshalled up, with their engines in steam, and one after another they followed up the empty carriage line, and into the station. In 12-coach loads at a time those vast crowds were cleared. Fortunately the only casualties were cases of fainting and exhaustion. No flying bomb fell anywhere near Paddington during the fearful three hours that the station was closed. No praise is enough for Sir James Milne and his senior officers for so anticipating requirements, and to all the operating men and footplate crews for working so assiduously beforehand to ensure everything was ready when the word to go was given.

Kay reported the incident in a carefully worded editorial note in *The Railway Gazette* of 4 August, 1944, thus:

Holiday Rush Closes Paddington Station

For the first time in its history Paddington Station had to be closed for three hours last Saturday morning, the platforms and "Lawn" being packed with would-be travellers. Soon approaches were densely crowded, and bookings had to be suspended from the Underground and tubes to prevent more passengers emerging from the subways and adding to the crowds in the main-line station. There was similar congestion at Euston and Waterloo and other stations, but not quite to the same extent as at Paddington. It is regrettable that, notwithstanding its competence in other directions, the Ministry of War Transport has not shone in its dealings with passenger rail travel. The same trouble has occurred at every holiday period during the war. Whilst refusing consistently to take any step to ration travel, it failed to give the railways a free hand to cope with any situation that might arise. It has contented itself with appeals and admonitions regarding unnecessary travel, apparently hoping that a Government Department could accomplish what no one else has succeeded in doing, namely getting a quart into a pint pot.

The trouble about the whole thing was that some 90 per cent of those who endured that agonising wait inside or outside the station on that dreadful Saturday would undoubtedly have put all the blame on the Great Western Railway. Hearing details of these events from the two friends who were particularly involved I could not help recalling the gracious words of Lord Greenwood, a guest at the Centenary Lunch at Bristol in 1935 when he said: 'All England seems to have a friendly family feeling for the Great Western', and wondering how those who stood for so long inside and outside Paddington in July 1944 would have felt!

In the last year of the war I saw a lot of Kay. Willox had resigned in 1942, and as a wartime expediency the veteran technical editor, Charles S. Lake, although 70 years of age, was asked to act additionally as Assistant Editor of both *The Railway Gazette* and *The Railway Magazine*. But he died at the end of the year, and both journals were without an assistant editor for many months. At the end of 1944 Kay asked me if I would like the dual job, Associate Editor of *The Railway Gazette*, and Editor-in-chief of *The Railway Magazine*. It would of course be a post war appointment, and his offer was left in abeyance. Meanwhile I was invited to join him on a number of occasions, so far as my own work with Westinghouse permitted. It gave me a rare insight into the personality of the man who had guided the fortunes of *The Railway Gazette* for 40 years, and the power he had exercised so skilfully and unobtrusively in presenting the railways' case, and especially that of the Great Western. I do not think he ever attended a GWR Board meeting as a visitor, but he was so much in the confidence of directors and officers alike that he might well have done. After the war my own circumstances changed so markedly that I felt compelled to decline his invitation to join his staff. My association with him was however an illuminating and very pleasant interlude in my business life. He died in 1949, at the early age of 67.

8
The Wivelscombe Rock Fall

By the winter of 1942 the people of Plymouth and its neighbourhood were used to war alarms. Hardened by the damage and grievous loss of life in the fearfully sustained bombing raids early in 1941, and the atmosphere of almost continuous alert, if not necessarily under 'raid imminent' warnings, a temporary blockage of the Cornish main line west of Saltash, and a period of single line working would have passed almost unnoticed. Tip and run air raids were nothing compared to the apocalyptic nights of March and April 1941. A brief interruption of traffic could have been due to the discovery of an unexploded bomb near to the line. After all, in the very week when I was drafting this chapter, April 1983, one of them was fished out of the River Thames, at Westminster! So, the incident of 8 December 1942 might have passed into the realm of things dealt with very much as a matter of routine in those wartime years had it not been for John Kay's intimate friendship with so many chief officers of the Great Western Railway, and his editorial nose for an interesting story. It was, in fact, very far indeed from a routine job. For security reasons news of the obstruction of an important main line could not be released until some time after the damage had been repaired, but then, in May 1944, an account of exceptional interest appeared in *The Railway Gazette*. At the time I remember Kay telling me that the Chief Engineer, then Sir Allan Quartermaine, lent him the complete set of confidential files covering the entire episode, and the description subsequently published was compiled by one of Kay's staff, from this fully authoritative information. To this account, necessarily coldly factual, I am indebted for details included in this present chapter.

Half-way along the four mile stretch between the now-demolished Defiance Halt and St Germans station is the $\frac{1}{4}$ mile long Wivelscombe Tunnel. It was then on a relatively new stretch of the Cornish main line, dating from 1905. Between Saltash and St Germans Brunel originally took the single-track Cornwall Railway nearer to the banks of the Lynher River, and between Wearde Quay, where the line turns away from the Tamar, and St Germans there were no fewer than five timber trestle viaducts, all of which would require replacement when the line was converted to double track. Instead of rebuilding the viaducts a deviation was built carrying the line further inland, and requiring only three new viaducts, at Forder, near Trematon Castle, and at St Germans itself, over the River Tiddy. The country just inland is hilly, which Brunel avoided by going nearer to the tidal creeks, and the crest of the hill beneath which the tunnel is carried is more than 200ft above sea level. The cutting on the eastern approach to the tunnel is no less than 80ft deep, and at the hilltop immediately above the tunnel there is a road junction of five country lanes, where that from Saltash leads to several isolated farmsteads.

It was to this lonely spot, late at night and feeling her way in the black-out, that Mrs W. Steer, drove her car. Her home, Wivelscombe Farm, was approached by little more than a cart track over the fields, and in the darkness, at 11pm on a December night, she was driving with extreme caution when suddenly she was aware of a sensation that the ground was moving beneath her. She stopped the car and got out to find that a 20yd length of the road had dropped about 4ft, and that cracks in the ground were opening all around her. In such intimidating circumstances, in the eerie darkness of the blacked out countryside, Mrs Steer could well have been excused had she panicked, and made her way to home, and hopefully to safety; but this intrepid lady thought instead of the nearness of the railway to this strange movement of the ground, and immediately found her way to the nearest telephone and reported her fears to the GWR at Plymouth. Her presence of mind in this emergency was such that she was able to pinpoint the exact time at which she felt the earth-movement under her car, as 11.09pm. Her telephone call received instant attention. All traffic was stopped, and the engineering department alerted. There was a freight train in the section, which of course could not be stopped, but it got through safely.

In view of such a report there could be no waiting for daylight to see what effect such a disturbance could have had on the railway. Without a very long detour to the north it was not possible to get there by road, because the Tamar ferries were not operating in

darkness during the war, but a senior member of the Divisional
Engineer's staff commandeered a locomotive and was at the site
before midnight. Even in the darkness he could see enough to know
that Mrs Steer's fears for the safety of the railway were well
founded, and that a great bulge in the side of the cutting
immediately east of the tunnel mouth had obstructed the down line.
The immediate stop on train movement imposed when the first
warning was received was upheld and the traffic department was
advised that the blockage of the line might be a lengthy one.
Immediately arrangements for a bus service to ferry passengers
were inaugurated, and negotiations opened for the routing of some
through freight trains over the North Cornwall line of the Southern
Railway, via Launceston and Wadebridge. When daylight came it
was seen that an enormous volume of *rock* was involved in the
movement, so extensive indeed that if further slips occurred the
entire width of this deep cutting could be obstructed. Blockage at
this part of the line caused considerable surprise to the engineers,
because of the apparent stability of the rock formation. No trouble
of any kind had been experienced since the construction of the
deviation line in 1905–7.

The cutting was in rock, with steep sides rough trimmed to slopes
of about 1 vertical to $\frac{3}{4}$ horizontal. The rock hereabouts is very slaty
in what is known as the Upper Devonian formation. It is
fascinating to the geologist in its folded and fractured nature,
giving clear evidence of some violent convulsions in the far-
prehistoric formation of the countryside, but regarded as
essentially stable in our own times. Yet when examination came to
be made of the disturbance that occurred on the night of 8–9
December, it was seen that the rock formation had been
considerably contorted, and that some of the beds were standing
nearly vertical and inclined slightly towards the railway. To an
untutored layman it might have seemed that there had been a slight
throw-back to the primeval convulsions that had formed this
countryside, millions of years ago.

Examination on the morning of 9 December 1942, showed that
for a length of about 70yd the more or less vertical strata of rock
forming the side of the cutting had fallen over towards the railway.
At the foot of the slope the large slabs of rock that had previously been vertical, had fallen over and were lying almost
horizontally and fouling the down main line. The same kind of
movement had occurred all the way up the slope, and the whole

cutting face supported precariously on the lowest slabs had bulged about 12ft beyond the original profile, and looked thoroughly unstable.

It was not surprising that Mrs Steer had been alarmed when her car began to be carried sideways, and that her pocket torch revealed so many cracks appearing in the ground. On the morning afterwards it was seen that the disturbance extended back to about 60ft beyond the original top of the cutting, and that the ground level had dropped about 4ft. The boundary fence marking the extent of railway property had moved 20ft towards the line, and it was this sideways movement that she first felt before getting out of her car and seeing the many cracks in the ground. There were two lines of procedure immediately apparent, to clear up the mess, and make the line safe for the resumption of traffic, but perhaps even more immediate was to be sure that the disturbance would not continue, and more fracturing and overturning of the rock formation develop. It was rare that railway engineers were faced with such a problem, and it was indeed a welcome change from the tiresome job of clearing up after an enemy air raid to have to deal with some basic geology. But the immediate problem, apart from that of getting the line open to traffic as quickly as possible was to ensure that no further falls of rock took place. The up main line was still unaffected, and if conditions were at least stabilised single-line working could be initiated. To all outward appearances however the cutting slopes on the down side of the line looked so unstable that the whole side might come down at any time and swamp the entire railway.

The first and immediate decision was therefore to shake the toe of the slip, by explosive, to loosen and bring down any material that was inclined to disintegrate. At the same time there was a vast amount of loose surface that it was desirable to remove. Men and wagons were mobilised as quickly as possible from various parts of the Plymouth Division, including the very expert cliff gang normally engaged on maintenance work on the coastal section between Teignmouth and Dawlish, and who had wide experience in dealing with minor landslips. The assistance was also obtained, in men, materials and expertise from a local quarrying firm. The speed with which remedial measures were undertaken will be realised when I add that the first blasting operation was carried out no later than the afternoon of 10 December, less than two days after the slip had taken place. In this operation 12 holes were sunk into the rock at the toe of the slip where the slabs had fallen over, and were lying almost horizontally. These were packed with a total charge of about 220 lb of ammonal, and fired simultaneously by an electric exploder, as recommended by the quarrying firm, from their intimate acquaintance with rock conditions in the neighbourhood. The severe explosion shook up the rock at the toe of the slip, but had no apparent effect on the rocks higher up the slope.

Contrary to all expectations this seemed to suggest that despite all that happened on the night of 8 December conditions were a good deal more stable than had been supposed. The most careful examination of the whole cutting side was made by the Divisional Engineer and senior members of his staff, in company with the invaluable aid of the quarrying firm, and the conclusion was reached that no further serious movement was likely to take place without reasonable warning. The conditions of 8 December were not likely to be repeated, because there would be many men working on the site, and those from any distance like the Teignmouth cliff gang would be accommodated for both sleeping and messing in rail coaches stabled near at hand. There would be no difficulty in arranging for a look-out to be mounted during the night. And so, as early as the afternoon of 10 December it was decided that the up line was in no immediate danger, and could be used, subject to a speed restriction to 5mph. I should add however that during the early hours of 9 December, after the preliminary examination in the black-out had shown the up line to be unaffected, two goods and one passenger train had been permitted to pass through at 5mph; but the line had been totally closed from 10.15am on 9 December until the results of the blasting had been observed.

It was immediately appreciated that single-line working between Saltash and St Germans coupled with the very slow running past the site of the slip would bring serious delays on occasions, and the wartime freight traffic to Falmouth, in particular, was heavy. The decision was immediately taken to lay in facing crossovers a short distance before and after the obstruction, while leaving enough space on the down line for stabling the wagons needed for the removal of the dislodged earth and rock, and for the sleeping accommodation for the men brought from more distant locations. As the work was expected to extend over several months temporary signalboxes were installed, and full block signalling provided, linked with the permanent signalboxes at St Germans and Wearde.

It is indicative of the urgency in which restoration of normal traffic working was regarded, that this work, including the laying of the crossovers and their connections, signalling, and electric token apparatus over the short length of single line past the obstruction was completely finished, and in service, in no more than *five days*.

Looking now at the detail on that first morning after the slip occurred, it was clear that if such a condition of instability could have developed on a stretch of line hitherto completely free from any such trouble it was essential to set up a close watch for signs of any further movement. First a field telephone was installed at the site for communication with the nearest signalboxes and with the railway telephone system generally. Then an exploratory gully was cut into the middle of the slip and a cement plaster band about 6in deep was put on to the rock along one side of this gully. It was hoped that any further disturbance, however slight, would show itself at once by cracks in this plaster. Then came the blasting at the toe of the slip on the afternoon of 10 December, strong enough, it was hoped to loosen and dislodge any areas that were likely to remain dangerous. For some little time afterwards the watch on that detecting plaster was particularly keen, but apart from the suspicion of a movement on the following day nothing further was discerned, and the work of repair could begin with the assurance that the ground was stable again.

Nevertheless, apart from the lengthy and toilsome task of clearing up the mess, and trimming back the slope of the cutting to its original profile there was a natural curiosity to probe deeper into the affected area to try and find the cause of such an unexpected and potentially serious geological convulsion. Removal of the loose earth and fractured rock just beneath the surface began at the top of the slip in the fields beyond the original line of railway boundary, and the immediate resiting of the farm roadway on which Mrs Steer had been driving was of course one of the first requirements. This was diverted some little distance clear of the upper line of cleavage of the ground. Excavation of the loose material began at the eastern end of the slip proceeding through towards the west, or tunnel end to a depth of about 7ft. The excavator used had a $\frac{3}{8}$ cu yd bucket of the face-shovel type, and it worked to and fro across the affected area, until the surface had been cleared to the edge of the cutting. Three more layers were afterwards excavated, until a depth of about 20ft below the original level of the ground had been cleared, and they were down to firm solid material. This particular phase of the work involved the removal of some 9000 cu yd all of a loose shaly nature, and easily dug by the excavator. It was fortunate that two worked-out quarries were near at hand and 8000 cu yd of material was conveyed there by tipping lorries, and dumped.

While this work was being started on the nearly level ground at the top of the cutting the Divisional Engineer began investigations to try and ascertain how, and where this alarming rock-fall had originated. A gully 7ft wide was opened in the face of the cutting at the middle of the slip, and it was hoped that this would expose the seat of the disturbance. The gully was driven horizontally until it had penetrated about 40ft from the face of the cutting, but unfortunately it was still in disturbed rock, and it was considered to be too costly to continue further in this way. But it was essential to discover the seat of the trouble, and it was decided to drive a tunnel heading 4ft wide by about 5ft high, downwards on a slope of 1 in 3 which penetrated hard slate saturated with moisture. At a distance inwards and downwards of about 18ft it seemed that stable conditions were being reached, and at 24ft the end of the heading presented solid rock. What was more important however, the sides and roof of the heading showed clearly the line of fracture with water constantly dripping from it.

In wet wintry weather the situation was complicated and obscured by rain falling into the open gully and running down into the sloping tunnel to where the line of fracture of the rock had been eventually located, and steps had to be taken to prevent rain entering. The extent of the water dripping from the line of fracture could then be accurately gauged. It was found that in wet weather seepage from the fracture filled the bottom of the heading to a depth of about 2ft; it never became more, even in times of very heavy rain, crevices in the disturbed rock provided an outlet that was equal to maximum inflow in the most severe conditions. Meanwhile a second open gully had been cut horizontally from rail level to try and find the base of the disturbance. The engineers did not have to cut in so far in this location to find the evidence they needed, and the line of fracture was discovered at only 35ft from the outer rail of the down line, and about 4ft above it. By pin-pointing the line of fracture at two places, and plotting them on a cross-sectional drawing of the ground the engineers were able to draw what were believed to be fairly accurate conclusions as to the complete nature of this extraordinary rock movement. It was believed that the pivot point was very close to the innermost point of the top heading, and that the rock had fractured along an almost vertical line to the original surface of the ground, about 35ft above. The rock strata towards the railway had then folded over to an angle of about 45 degrees, leaving a triangular void into which the ground away from the railway subsided, taking the farm roadway and Mrs Steer and her car with it.

The folding of the rock strata, and the associated movement lower down pushed out the side of the cutting into a jagged, irregular profile well beyond the original, and at its lower end giving every impression of being about to topple over and completely block both lines. However the blasting operation on 10 December did much to lessen such fears. Nevertheless, at the time of the incident more than 35 years had passed since the Wearde – St Germans deviation line had been built, without the slightest sign of any weakness in the formation, and those responsible for the maintenance of the line and the safety of traffic could well have continued to ponder as to the root cause of the rock fracture. While very heavy bombing on targets east of the Tamar had occurred during the early spring of the previous year the concentrated target area lay some four to six miles to the east and the weight of individual bombs then used by the enemy in those attacks would not have been likely to cause disturbance to the rock strata, and by a delayed action of more than 18 months. The mystery remains, especially as another 40 years have now passed since the incident, with not the slightest sign of further trouble.

Meanwhile, all theorising apart, plans had to be made for the clearance of the vast amount of rock and earth that had been loosened, and which still threatened to tumble down and block the cutting. The first thing was to provide for a loading platform just above the toe of the slip from which railway wagons could be loaded. To build this, to minimise the disturbance at the top both down and up lines were slewed away from the slip by about 2ft, which was as much as the clearance on the opposite bank of the cutting would permit. The platform was then constructed to overhang the side of the rail tip wagons standing on the down line, and built with sufficient slope to help the run of the debris towards the wagons. The loading platform was completed by 25 January 1943, and the excavation at the top of the slip had by that time reached the stage when it was considered safe to begin dislodging the edges of rock which stuck out beyond the line of the debris. This is where the expertise of the cliff gang was invaluable, for this work was done by men suspended by ropes, and using air drills.

The 7ft wide gully previously mentioned, and driven 40ft horizontally into the face of the slip, had confirmed the view that it would be safe if the cutting slope was trimmed back to an inclination of 1 to 1, and the main phase of the excavation then began. It was indeed significant of the seriousness with which the incident was regarded that nearly six weeks elapsed before the principal remedial operations began. But since the completion of the temporary crossovers and the signalling associated with them on 18 December, the full traffic of the line had been flowing, both passenger and goods, albeit at no more than 5mph. The first step towards the trimming of the new cutting face was to cut gullies 7ft wide and 30ft apart to the required new profile, to serve as guides for the excavation. The piled up material between the gullies was then removed, and the gullies themselves, used as chutes to carry the debris to the loading platforms at the bottom, and so into the waiting tip wagons standing on the down line. This was a long and arduous operation involving the continuous employment of 50 men.

Blasting was necessary to dislodge the more compact blocks and a powder specially suited to the type of rock was necessary. The charges were fired by slow burning fuses, and it was of course necessary to arrange blasting at times when no trains were expected. This was not always easy, because the incidence of heavy wartime special traffic occasioned long delays, even to the regularly scheduled passenger trains, not to mention the freights. As a precaution the electric token for the short single-line section past the slip was withdrawn at these times, and the token held by the foreman in charge until blasting was completed, and subsequent inspection showed that no debris had fallen on the line. After debris from the face of the cutting was loaded into the wagons on the down line they were shunted a short distance out of the cutting and unloaded down a steep embankment. For economy in labour a set of eight side-tip wagons was used, each capable of holding 15 cu yd. In all some 3000 cu yd of material was cleared in this way, and it was not until May, 1943, that the site was cleared and the cutting slope correctly trimmed.

Normal double line working was restored on Sunday 2 May, with a speed restriction of 5mph on both lines. That on the up line was removed after a fortnight, to the normal limit of 60mph that had applied to the entire Cornish main line for many years previously, and which was not relaxed until comparatively recent times. The 5mph restriction on the down line was however enforced for some months further in 1943, while observation and further site investigation continued. The crossover roads and the temporary signalboxes, though no longer used, were retained in position, in case there should be any repetition of instability in the coming winter. Happily none came; but I must admit to cocking a weather-eye at that cutting slope as we approached Wivelscombe Tunnel on the many footplate runs I have made over the route since 1946. Nowadays the HSTs go through that cutting and tunnel at 70 to 75mph.

9

The Locomotive Department under Hawksworth

In the 1930s when the privilege of riding on the footplate of locomotives in traffic was being accorded to me by a number of railways, including the Northern of France, the Great Western was not yet among their number. Towards the end of the war however I had made contact with the American railway magazine *Trains*, and its editor suggested that an article describing current locomotive working conditions on British railways would be welcomed. This was an attractive enough idea in itself, but in the autumn of 1944 not too easy so far as getting the necessary data was concerned. In my ordinary daily duties I was then working 6½ days a week, with a completely free Saturday once a month. The London area was still plagued with flying bombs, and V2 rocket attacks, but the north to west expresses of the GWR, with some turns still worked as prestige double-home turns by Newton Abbot and Shrewsbury sheds, seemed a fair proposition. I could travel to either starting point on the Friday night before one of my free Saturdays and make the through trip on the following day. F. W. Hawksworth had succeeded Collett as Chief Mechanical Engineer in 1941, and to him I wrote for the necessary authority to ride on the footplate.

In complete contrast to the brusque refusal I had received from Collett to a request I had made in 1935, permission was readily granted in 1944, and in conditions of such courtesy from the running inspectors deputed to ride with me and such friendliness in correspondence, both before and after, that I was made to feel thoroughly welcome. I wrote a two-instalment article for the American journal, and followed it with a similar one requested by John Kay for *The Railway Magazine*. Swindon was apparently pleased with the results, but, so I learned many years later, found the details of some of the hill-climbing I described a little too good to be believed. They had no data in the office over that route ready to hand for comparison, and because dynamometer car tests were prohibited in wartime a small team from the testing section of the drawing office was sent out to check on the trains by which I had travelled. They returned to Swindon to report that some of the hill-climbing was even better than mine, and I gathered that from then onwards anything I recorded was accepted without any question. Actually the climbing from Shrewsbury up to Church Stretton, which had caught the eye of the authorities at Swindon, was not nearly as good as I had logged with the same engine, Castle class 4–6–0 No 5072 on the same train when travelling as a passenger in 1940. The engine was then named *Compton Castle*, but was renamed *Hurricane* later in 1940. Whereas on my footplate run speed on the lengthy 1 in 90–100 gradients between Dorrington and Church Stretton had come down to a steady 28mph – good work nevertheless with a 450-ton load – in 1940 the minimum speed had been 34mph with 445 tons.

From that opening acquaintance with the running inspectors of the GWR I had many privileges. I was introduced to Hawksworth himself one day at Paddington, when I had been lunching with Major Dewar, the Publicity Officer, and the animated conversation that followed on all kinds of locomotive topics led to my missing the train I intended catching! I met him many times subsequently, sometimes by appointment, others like that memorable lecturing occasion at the Swindon Engineering Society referred to in Chapter 6, by chance. There was one topic however, I was warned beforehand never to raise with him, and that was his proposed express passenger 4–6–2 design. It was a very sore point with him, and his reaction when he heard that another railway author, after receiving a sniff of the grape vine, had tried by caballistic methods to extract some authoritative information out of the drawing office had been dramatic. Although Hawksworth had then retired he went into the drawing office, asked for the drawings concerned and promptly destroyed them all, with his own hands. He once referred to the incident when talking to me, though not mentioning the actual object of the 'illegal' attempt to get information. Although it had happened some months previously, in referring, still in deep indignation, to the man concerned, he said to me: 'You don't do things like that!'

I have told of my contacts with two of his staff, F. C. Mattingley, and J. W. Innes, in connection with the GWR form of the vacuum brake to be fitted to the post-war coaches built at Gloucester, but the men concerned with locomotives included some colourful characters. When I was doing my first footplate work his principal assistant, and deputy head of the CME's department was Fred Hall, a most charming personality who I never saw without a benevolent smile on his face. He initialled the letters giving me my first footplate authorities, and always had some cheery postcript to add in manuscript to the formal letters. In later years his younger brother became Divisional Motive Power Superintendent at Newton Abbot and continued in the same friendly family tradition towards me. Bill Pellow, who was then Outdoor Assistant to the CME and Locomotive Running Superintendent, was a Cornishman, with a dry sense of humour. Hawksworth, still smarting from the disappointment of having his Pacific project vetoed was rather wary about the introduction of his County class two-cylinder 4–6–0, which included two design features intended for the Pacific – 6ft 3in coupled wheels, and 280 lb/sq in in boiler pressure. Pellow, who after all would have to use the new 4–6–0s, had not been told much about them, and was a bit up-stage when Hawksworth invited him to see the first one completed, No 1000. Walking to see it with Hawksworth, in his dry Cornish way he said: 'What is it, a shunting engine?'

All the locomotive running inspectors reported to Pellow, and in all the footplate work I have done in this country and abroad I have never come across a body of men who were held in such esteem, both by the technical staff at Swindon headquarters, and by the drivers and firemen out on the line. I think that very happy situation came from the days of G. J. Churchward, who always regarded the running inspectors as his eyes and ears. They came to know that serious attention was always given in the drawing office to reports they put in, of difficulties or failings with engines, both as classes and as individual machines, while the footplatemen, from long experience looked upon them as their friends, to whom they could confide troubles. Only once in the thousands of miles I have ridden on engines of Great Western design have I seen an altercation between a driver and an inspector. That was on a very sick engine, and the dispute was over how best to nurse it along. In that particular case I felt sure that the driver was right.

When I made my first Great Western footplate journeys Alex Cameron was Chief Inspector, but I did not meet him until I rode down on the Cornish Riviera Express, or rather its austerity equivalent, in the early summer of 1947. On my earlier trips I had ridden with Vercoe, from Newton Abbot, Bill Davies, Bristol, Harris from Wolverhampton, and Charles Pullen, a headquarters man who succeeded Cameron as Chief Inspector. All had been top link enginemen themselves, and the older ones, like Vercoe and Harris, wore the traditional bowler hat. The younger ones came to wear less conventional and more comfortable headgear. They were a tremendous help to me, and often to the enginemen also. In those immediate post-war years we often had poor coal, and firemen who were not as experienced as the particular duty needed. Then an inspector who was prepared to take the shovel for a few spells, and show a young man how it should be done was a friend indeed. I made a number of trips during the period when oil firing was being used, and the degree to which the changed techniques of firing had been mastered was impressive to watch. I rode on some hard turns, such as the Cornish Riviera Express each way between Plymouth and Penzance, and one of the fastest Bristol trains. My footplate experience extended for many years into British Railways days; but the Great Western tradition persisted even to the extent of trying to get the best out of the new BR standard locomotives, which at times was *not* easy!

While, as can be appreciated from the foregoing, my earlier contacts with the locomotive department of the GWR were with the footplatemen my later, more significant, and lasting associations were with the technical staff in the drawing office, and particularly those of the testing section. Above all, in 1946–7, there was A. W. J. Dymond, Assistant to the Chief Mechanical Engineer, who was then deeply involved with the introduction of the first gas turbine locomotive. Jack Dymond was a brilliant technologist, but for all that a born railwayman with a wealth of outdoor experience behind him in many divisional posts before he was chosen by Hawksworth as his special technical assistant. In his earlier drawing office days he had the job of laying out the design of the special bogie fitted to the King class locomotives. The senior draughtsman on the locomotive side was then G. E. Scholes, but alone among Swindon men I did not find him very communicative, or very enthusiastic about the great old railway. He was inclined to regard the present situation as antiquated – to use his own words. It might have been me that put him off, but I was glad when he took me along to the testing section of the drawing office, and introduced me to the inimitable Sam Ell. For there, in him and every member of his staff I found enthusiasm at bubbling-over point.

Dynamometer car testing, and responsibility for the stationary testing plant was always a function of the locomotive drawing office on the Great Western Railway. When I first had the privilege of meeting this splendid band of young engineers they were engaged in testing the first of the King class engines to be fitted with a high degree superheater. Before I went down to see the stationary plant in action Hawksworth had explained to me why he was breaking away from the Churchward tradition of a moderate degree of superheat. He felt that with the greatly varying qualities of coal they then had to accept it would give the driver a better chance when conditions were bad. Although he did not mention the LMS there is no doubt that since Stanier went there his work had been very closely watched at Swindon, and his acceptance of the view that the Great Western precepts of superheating were not applicable to the varied conditions of fuel, and of footplate expertise between Shoeburyness and Wick had been carefully noted. This, of course, merely bore out what C. J. Bowen Cooke had been aware of, from his long experience of running conditions, when he introduced superheating on the London & North Western Railway as long previously as 1910. While Hawksworth told me he agreed that with a high degree of superheat, when things were going well some heat was thrown away in the exhaust, any theoretical disadvantage in this respect was worth sustaining in view of the more reliable working when things were difficult.

While varying qualities of coal had been part of the way of life on other railways, even well before the war, it had not been so on the Great Western, and even by the year 1947 the men had still not accepted it as one of those things. I shall always remember a conversation at Exeter shed. I had been footplating in Cornwall in the friendly company of Charles Pullen. My family was on holiday at Teignmouth, and after finishing my official trip at Plymouth, on the up Cornish Riviera, he had suggested that we rode a County class 4–6–0 non-stop to Exeter on the Wolverhampton train, and that I made my way back to Teignmouth on a local. With no more than the Cornish part of the train, except for the brief poundings up the Hemerdon and Dainton banks, it was an easy job, though with a mixture of indifferent coal and ovoids the engine had not steamed too well. However, the County was going no further than Exeter, where combination with the Torquay line portion of the train put a Castle in spanking condition at the head for the through working to Wolverhampton. I was walking round the shed yard with

Pullen, taking some photographs, when the running foreman came up. After enquiring politely how we fared coming up from Plymouth, and noting the fuel on our engine, he turned on my companion and said: 'What *are* we to do with such coal?' 'Burn it!' came the immediate reply. The running foreman shrugged his shoulders and said: 'You can't. It's b—— well incombustable!'

The first King to have high degree superheat, No 6022, was running on the stationary test plant when I first saw it and met Sam Ell; his assistant then was another ebullient character, 'Chick' Ockwell, and the two of them took me round every feature that was under examination. Any visitor to an engineering plant in action is always the object of some curiosity to the men employed, but on this first acquaintance with Ell's team I was impressed by the friendliness and enthusiasm of all concerned, even to the top link driver and fireman working away on the footplate as if they were out on the line hauling a heavy express train. For the young engineers engaged on the numerous quantities to be observed and recorded it was a welcome change from the monastic-like calm of the drawing office, particularly with prospects of confirmatory tests with the dynamometer car out on the line. But on the Great Western the drawing office was the most usual channel of promotion to higher things. Sam Ell, at one stage in his career, had followed in the footsteps of Hawksworth himself, and just as the CME had taken great pride in making the general arrangement drawing of *The Great Bear*, so similarly it had fallen to Ell to make the general arrangement drawing of the King. I have often wondered if it were not Hawksworth's early association with 'The Bear' that fired his ambition to have a Pacific of his own in later years.

Sam Ell was an artist as well as a draughtsman, a caricaturist into the bargain. In the archives at Swindon there used to be an album of his drawings recording the lighter side of life in the loco-motive drawing office, and its outside activities. One (*opposite*) shows the 'Trials of the Barbary Castle in BC Umpteen'. The drawing was made in 1926, long before the Great Western had an engine named *Barbury Castle*, and showed his then-boss in the drawing office, C. K. Dumas, in the garb of an Ancient Briton riding astride the pre-historic monster taking indicator diagrams! Dumas was a widely-read and well-travelled man, as well as being a first class experimental engineer. He contributed a most comprehensive and scholarly article to *The Railway Magazine* in

Great Western motive power on test in B.C. Umpteen

1926 on 'Testing Locomotive Engines'. The practices described, while essentially basic, related entirely to the GWR, though no mention of this was made in the text; but with one exception all the many photographs illustrating the article were taken at the time of the full dress trials of *Caldicot Castle* between Swindon and Plymouth in March 1924. The article gives, however, not a glimmer of the immense personality and impish sense of humour of the writer. At the time Hawksworth was Chief Draughtsman, with responsibility for all experimental work and testing, and without any doubt that article would have had to pass his lynx-eyed scrutiny before it was submitted for publication. Ell caught the lighter side of those test occasions with the *Caldicot Castle*, which involved three return trips to Plymouth, with a cartoon entitled 'Ready for the Double-home'. It shows Dumas packing his bag, a tattered old Gladstone, with a night-shirt, and the maximum number of bottles of beer that he could stuff in – nothing more!

One of the most intriguing features of the Hawksworth era at Swindon was the way in which certain major points of design, which had been considered sacrosanct since the early days of Churchward, had immediately been thrown overboard, by a man who had probably more experience than any one else in their detail features, and their record in service, maintenance and repair charges. I refer particularly to the Swindon superheater. The Schmidt superheater had been discarded after a trial on one engine,

115

no doubt partly to avoid having to pay royalties on a proprietary article, but at the same time to render the elements more easily removable. But Churchward's adaptation of the American Cole type, to form the celebrated Swindon superheater, included flat metal-to-metal joints between the elements and header, which needed careful fitting, and careful maintenance to keep them steam tight. Not long after Hawksworth had become Chief Mechanical Engineer, the Great Western was required by the Government to build a batch of Stanier 2–8–0s of the LMS standard 8F class. They had the Derby variation of the Schmidt superheater, with the regulator in the dome, and it was not long before Swindon, building these engines, appreciated how much easier it was to make a good job of the joint between the elements and the header than on their own type. The insularity and isolationism that had surrounded Swindon design practice since Collett's time was being penetrated and on the first new engines for which Hawksworth was responsible, the 6959 class of Hall, the superheater was redesigned on the LMS pattern but retaining the regulator valve in the smokebox. These engines, put into traffic in 1944, won golden opinions on every account, and the first postwar batch of Castles, introduced in May 1946 had superheaters of a similar design.

When I first met Ell and his gang they had been busy running trials, both on the stationary plant and with the dynamometer car, with three varieties of Castle: one of the original standard type with the two-row Swindon superheater, one of the 1946 batch, and an engine that had been fitted with a four-row superheater, similar to that on King class engine No 6022. The three Castles concerned were No 5087 *Tintern Abbey*, which had been rebuilt with a Castle boiler from one of the Abbey series of Stars; the first of the 1946 engines, No 5098 *Clifford Castle*; and No 5049 *Earl of Plymouth*. No 5098 was not really a true representative of the three-row superheater class, because it and its sister engine, 5099 had the old standard sight-feed lubricator, whereas all those from 7000 upwards had a mechanical lubricator new to Great Western practice. There were always variations between individual engines, but lubricators apart No 5098 was an outstandingly good one. It was used for some of the prestige Ocean Mail specials from Plymouth, and I had a splendid run on its footplate when working the 9.45am West to North express through from Newton Abbot to Shrewsbury. From what the testing staff told me I gathered that as far as power output and coal consumption were concerned the three-cornered contest between engines 5087, 5098 and 5049 gave inconclusive results, but the 5098 class, as the three-row superheater variety was officially known, was generally favoured for shed and works purposes.

No 5098 was the third Castle to bear the name *Clifford Castle*. It had previously been on 5046, and then 5071. The circumstances in which it was first displaced, together with those on Nos 5043–5062 inclusive, were rather amusing. In 1936 many 4–4–0 engines of the Duke class were nearing the end of their useful lives, and replacements were needed for working over the former Cambrian main line, from Oswestry through to the coast. Weight restrictions were severe, and Bulldog class 4–4–0s could not be used, so Swindon produced a hybrid, rebuilding 20 of the Bulldogs with Duke class domed boilers. It was at first proposed to perpetuate the names of the Duke class 4–4–0s that had been replaced; but then, following the system of class nomenclature, someone suggested naming them after Earls, all living personalities, either directors, or otherwise connected with the Great Western Railway. The first of the hybrids was named *Earl of Mount Edgcumbe*, and 19 other names were selected. The work of rebuilding and naming had proceeded as far as the thirteenth engine, completed at Swindon in May 1937, and then suddenly all the names were removed. The story goes that at least one of the eminent gentlemen, intended to be honoured by having his name on an engine, took strong objection to it being used on so relatively humdrum a class, and kicked up hell! In consequence all the Earl names were removed from the 3200 class 4–4–0s, and put instead on to the 5043–5062 batch of Castles. The original *Clifford Castle* thereupon became *Earl Cawdor*. A new batch of Castles, 5068–5082, was programmed for 1938–9, and *Clifford Castle* was allocated to No 5071; but the name was carried for no more than two years, for in 1940, in honour of the undying fame achieved by the RAF in the Battle of Britain, No 5071, in company with nine other Castles were renamed after the aircraft involved, and 5071 became *Spitfire*.

The tests to which the third and final bearer of the name *Clifford Castle* was submitted, in 1946, were among the first conducted on Great Western locomotives that embodied the more precise methods of examination conceived in the later 1930s, when the hit or miss nature of the older traditional methods with the dynamometer car were being more truly appreciated. This process of evolution, for which a young draughtsman attached to the

testing section, C. T. Roberts, was mainly responsible, arose in a
rather roundabout way. In the early 1930s, following the record
running of the Cheltenham Flyer in 1932, the civil engineer's
department, always a bit touchy on the subject of maximum speeds,
seems to have had its doubts about the way speed restrictions were
being observed on the West of England route, and asked Swindon
to submit a chart showing the actual speeds, maximum and
minimum, to maintain the current schedule of the Cornish Riviera
Express. The normal winter loading was 500 tons tare to Westbury,
430 tons on to Taunton, and 360 tons to Plymouth, and the booked
point-to-point times, and the associated average speeds were thus:

Distance Miles		Booked Time min	Average speed m.p.h.
0.0	Paddington	0	—
9.1	Southall	11	49.6
18.5	Slough	20	62.7
36.0	Reading	36	65.7
53.1	Newbury	54	57.0
66.4	Bedwyn	67	61.4
94.6	Heywood Rd Junc	94	64.2
115.1	Castle Cary	$112\frac{1}{2}$	66.5
140.3	Creech Junc	$135\frac{1}{4}$	66.2
142.7	Taunton	138	57.6
173.5	Exeter	169	59.6

With the data from the 1927 dynamometer car test runs with
engine No 6005 before him, and a few runs on the footplate it did
not take Charles Roberts long to decide that the existing point-to-
point timings of the Cornish Riviera were quite unrealistic in
places, in making uneven demands upon the boiler, if accurately
maintained. But of course, as he saw on the footplate, drivers were
not attempting to keep the sharpest, and most impractical of the
intermediate times, and were steaming their engines at an
approximately constant rate regaining minutes lost on the easier
sections. There was no difficulty in keeping overall time to the
critical points, such as Heywood Road Junction, where the
Weymouth slip coaches were detached, or to Taunton.

In preparing the speed graphs required by the Chief Engineer, and in comparing the results with some of the test data that had been obtained with No 6005 there began to emerge a more scientific concept of train timing, based on a constant rate of evaporation in the boiler. This would not only yield more economical performances, but would probably make things easier for the fireman. The drawing office had not progressed very far with this project, when the traffic department, following the introduction of the 1¾ hour Bristolian service in 1935, began to consider possibilities for a similar service to Birmingham. The distance from Paddington was eight miles less than Bristol, and would involve an average speed of no more than 63.2mph if made non-stop. The locomotive department was asked what it could do about it, with the proviso that the load should be one of eight coaches, or about 300 tons. The Chief Engineer then added his stipulation that the maximum speed must on no account exceed 80mph. In view of what was regularly run on the Birmingham line, and had been run ever since the restoration of the 2-hour trains in the Autumn of 1921, this was unrealistic in the extreme, and rather suggested that his department had not a clue as to what was run every day of the week at locations such as Haddenham, and Fosse Road going down, and at Warwick, Blackthorn, and Denham coming up.

When it came to the preparation of a speed chart of the 1¾-hour express from Paddington to Birmingham, Swindon drawing office was equally in blinkers. Whether it had any actual running data for the route with Star, Castle or King class engines is doubtful. I have not heard of any dynamometer test runs being made, probably because when the new route was opened in 1910 the loads of the 2-hour trains were at first so light that no difficulty was envisaged in keeping time. Saint class two-cylinder 4–6–0s were principally employed, and so far as high speed was concerned the service had not long been in operation before a maximum of 90mph was recorded by Cecil J. Allen, and published with much *éclat* in *The Railway Magazine*. I did not hear of any repercussions on this, and can only assume that the magazine was not then read in the offices of the Chief Engineer! Whether it was *really* believed in the 1930s that the service was being run without exceeding 80mph is hard to imagine. Quite apart from maximum speed however Swindon drawing office found itself constrained in a more serious way when setting out to produce its speed graphs.

The only basic data it had to hand relating to the performance of

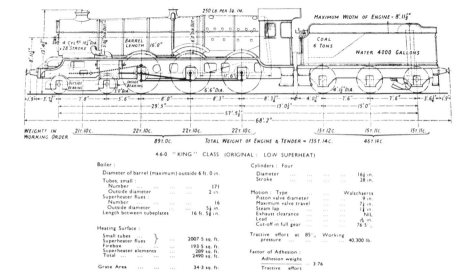

4-6-0 "KING" CLASS (ORIGINAL : LOW SUPERHEAT)

Boiler :				Cylinders : Four				
Diameter of barrel (maximum) outside 6 ft. 0 in.				Diameter			16¼ in.	
Tubes, small :				Stroke			28 in.	
Number			171					
Outside diameter ...			2 in.	Motion : Type			Walschaerts	
Superheater flues :				Piston valve diameter ...			9 in.	
Number			16	Maximum valve travel ...			7¼ in.	
Outside diameter ...			5¼ in.	Steam lap			1¼ in.	
Length between tubeplates			16 ft. 5¼ in.	Exhaust clearance ...			NIL.	
				Lead			7/32 in.	
Heating Surface :				Cut-off in full gear ...			76.5 %.	
Small tubes ... }								
Superheater flues			2007·5 sq. ft.	Tractive effort at 85%, Working				
Firebox			193·5 sq. ft.	pressure			40,300 lb.	
Superheater elements			289 sq. ft.					
Total			2490 sq. ft.	Factor of Adhesion :				
				Adhesion weight		... 3·76		
Grate Area			34·3 sq. ft.	Tractive effort				

the King class engines was that obtained in the 1927 trials of 6005, on runs between Swindon and Frome, via Reading West, and the Birmingham speed charts had to be based on the maximum steaming rate that could be sustained for any length of time by a single fireman. Roberts' precept of calculating times on the basis of a continuous rate of evaporation in the boiler was difficult to apply on this route, because of the sharp fluctuation in gradients, and the incidence of many speed restrictions below the overall imposed maximum of 80mph. Whether the locomotive running inspectors familiar with the route were consulted I do not know, but in the outcome the chart was as unlike average performance over the line as to be almost farcical. I have sometimes wondered if this was not another example of what was once referred to as C. B. Collett's 'diabolical cunning' when faced with something that he did not want to be involved in. The speed charts for a 1¾-hour run with a 300-ton train, and for a 2-hour run with 400 tons were published as large folding plates in *The Railway Gazette*, and to anyone who knew the route and its running, the difference between premise and actuality was just laughable. To quote one particular item: the 1¾-hour down train was shown as requiring 14½ minutes to cover the 16.2 miles from Northolt Junction to High Wycombe; I have logged it myself in 14min 55sec with Saint class 4—6—0 No 2906 *Lady of Lynn* hauling a load of 295 tons tare, an engine with a tractive effort not much more than *half* that of a King.

However the ideas of train timing at constant rates of evaporation may have been used, or misused, in presenting speed charts for the Birmingham line, they were developed to magnificent purpose after the war, when Sam Ell was in charge of the testing section of the drawing office. Both in private, and on certain engineering occasions, he always made the most generous acknowledgement to Charles Roberts for the original conception of the principle, though its full flowering did not occur until after the Great Western Railway itself had ceased to exist, and Hawksworth himself had retired. He had a great team in those immediate post-war years, and it would have been interesting to see how the CME's department would have developed had not nationalisation swamped everything in 1948. So far as engine testing was concerned, everything was at first subjugated to the interchange trials set up by the newly established Railway Executive, a long, expensive and inconclusive exercise conducted on the old hit or miss basis, with emphasis eventually on the miss. Hawksworth, naturally, was not particularly interested; but Ell, Ockwell, and their staff were very much involved because the Churchward dynamometer car was also used for all the Waterloo–Exeter test runs over the former Southern Railway, in addition to those over GW routes.

In the last year before nationalisation there had been some important changes among the senior staff. Fred Hall was retiring, and Kenneth Cook, who had been Locomotive Works Manager since Hannington's tragic death, became Principal Assistant to the CME. Hugh Randle, who had been Carriage & Wagon Works Manager, succeeded him in the Locomotive Works. The still relatively youthful Charles Roberts, was appointed Carriage & Wagon Works Manager, and Geoffrey Tew his assistant, previously at Paddington as Assistant to the Divisional Locomotive Superintendent, had looked after my interests on several occasions, including a very enjoyable visit to the extensive activities at Old Oak Common. Between them these four men alone spread Great Western influence far and wide after nationalisation. Randle became Carriage & Wagon Engineer of the London Midland Region, and Roberts, later, was Chief Mechanical & Electrical Engineer, Scottish Region. Tew went to Wolverton Carriage Works, as Manager, and received me very happily when I went there on an investigation into London & North Western carriage history. Jack Dymond remained at WR locomotive headquarters to be one of many 'inside', who carried on the old tradition initiated by Churchward himself, of undertaking civic duties, and eventually becoming Mayor of Swindon. But of them all it was Kenneth Cook that I knew best personally, and of his work after he transferred to the Eastern Region. It was, of course, through him and his installation of the optical system of lining up frames and axlebox centres that the Gresley Pacifics of both A3 and A4 classes were so magnificently rejuvenated, after the Thompson debacle, and saw steam out on the East Coast route.

I met Cook many times after he had left Swindon, once or twice in amusing circumstances. Despite the splendid work he did at Doncaster and Darlington I suppose it was only natural that his heart had remained in the West Country, and I remember a conversation with him and Sir William Stanier over a cup of tea, before a meeting of the Institution of Locomotive Engineers. Both were enthusing quietly over some detail of Great Western practice, and in a pause in the conversation Sir William said: 'Oh yes; we've all got GWR embroidered inside the seats of our trousers'. On another occasion, having been to York on some signalling work I was travelling south by the Heart of Midlothian, as the afternoon Scotsman was then named. We had made the regular passenger stop at Grantham, just as the down Yorkshire Pullman, which should have been non-stop from Kings Cross to Doncaster drew in to a halt; there, immediately opposite the dining car in which I was travelling were Kenneth Cook and his wife, Trixie. Within seconds windows were down and greetings shouted across. Rather ruefully he said 'We're short of steam' but at that moment we got the right-away. We did not start however, but went backwards instead for a few yards, the valves on our A1 Pacific evidently being 'blind'. When we got away properly, and were passing him he still had the window down and shouted across: 'Three cylinders don't start so well as four!'

I have always been as interested in the contrasting locomotive practice of the LNER as I am of the Great Western, but in conversation with Cook I was surprised to find that he consistently played down the importance of the work he did on the Gresley Pacifics, which I have always felt sure was quite invaluable, and will be regarded so by future locomotive historians. It is interesting to try and imagine how Great Western locomotive practice would have advanced had there been no nationalisation, and had he succeeded Hawksworth as Chief Mechanical Engineer in his own right, with the departmental set-up unchanged from earlier days, and all the traditional precepts to back him up. Would the Hawksworth or a Cook Pacific then have been built for the GWR?

10
Control – the GW way

There were times when one could have gained the impression that the Great Western management disliked crowds. Certainly its main line passenger coaches were designed for the transport of the maximum of passengers on a minimum of tare weight, at any rate to 1930; but they liked to have everything neat, tidy, and orderly. In the 19th century there was no encouragement for third class passengers to travel by the GWR. The crack expresses carried first and second class only, but in later years this situation, as emphasised in Chapter 4 of this book, swung the other way, and even on such a prestige train as the Cornish Riviera Express there was remarkably little in the way of *first* class accommodation. But the Great Western endeavoured to have everything planned, even at the busiest holiday times by encouraging everyone to reserve their seats in advance, so that it knew approximately how many people to expect, and how many extra coaches to add to the normal rakes of the various express trains. After that it was left, almost entirely, to the uniformed staff to get on with the job. The senior ranks were regarded as responsible men, who would need no guidance in carrying out the programmes devised by the 'higher ups'.

Earlier chapters of this book however have shown how catastrophically this operational philosophy could get out of gear, as at Christmas 1935. At the time of the flying bomb attack, in 1944 the situation was quite different, and arose from a loyal adherence to a Government decree made without any anticipation of what could arise in a sudden and unexpected situation of dire emergency. The crisis that developed at Paddington on that dramatic Saturday in late July was no fault of the Great Western management. But the appalling congestion, and the manner in which it was eventually cleared, remained graven on the heart of every operating man in the London Division; and when the end of the war brought the granting of holidays with pay, and the number of families seeking to get away for longer breaks than a day trip to the seaside, the summer holiday period began to take on an aspect never previously presented to the railways. Serving such a favoured holiday region as Devon and Cornwall the Great Western began to prepare to handle a lion's share of this new traffic.

There was, nevertheless, a vast difference from the holiday business on which the GWR had flourished before the war. The basic unchanging attitude of employers, and of those offering holiday accommodation remained – no variation from Saturday to Saturday bookings; but the attitudes of the passengers themselves had changed. Seat reservation during the war had ceased. Everyone, even senior business executives who *had* to travel, got used to scrumming in anywhere they could find a seat. Packing into the corridors, or even into the guard's vans became a way of life, and many of those who had to travel in those conditions, and who had hardly travelled at all before the war imagined it was the normal thing on the railways. When it came to holidays with pay their wives and children scrummed in with them, and looked forward to the time when they would be able to have a family car! While seat reservations were reintroduced on some trains soon after the war there were so many new travellers venturing on the holiday routes to the South West who did not make use of the facility that at times there was a fog of uncertainty as to how many people would present themselves to be conveyed from Paddington on summer Saturdays.

Then, as if the post-war situation was not difficult enough there came the coal crisis, in the midst of the terrible winter of 1946–7, and in March the government of the day instructed all the railways to curtail their services to save coal. One of the Great Western withdrawals to meet this demand was to take off the Cornish Riviera Express, and allow the 11am general service train to take its place. In the first week of the withdrawal the Member of Parliament for St Ives asked the Minister of Transport how much coal would be saved by taking off the Limited. The Minister himself, Alfred Barnes, of course had not a clue, but in a written reply he said about 110 tons a week. I do not think that Swindon would have been flattered by this figure, which suggested that the engines concerned, even on decelerated post war schedules would be using about 60 lb per mile. In any case it was a wholly Pyrrhic gesture, because the moment there was any extra traffic the Great Western put on relief trains ahead of it. In connection with some literary work on which I was then engaged F. W. Hawksworth gave me a footplate pass to ride the engine of the 11am down, on a Saturday it is true, and I found the train running in *five* portions! There were trains, all going to Newton Abbot or beyond, leaving at 10.30, 10.35, 10.40 and 10.55, with the 10.45 to Weston-super-Mare in the middle of this procession. On the 11am itself the whole 14-coach train (505 tons) was taken through to Plymouth, with stops at Taunton, Exeter, Dawlish, Teignmouth and Newton Abbot; an assisting engine was taken from there over the South Devon banks, and yet another intermediate stop was made at Brent.

On that occasion I had been concerned with the locomotive work, but on another very busy Saturday, just before the Whitsun Bank Holiday, I was given an insight into the passenger control on these occasions. Beginning on the Friday night a temporary control centre was set up in the very heart of things. This took the form of a saloon coach, fully equipped with telephones, berthed against the buffer stops in No 2 platform line at Paddington, at a convenient point for quick reception of messages from railway staff, from the police who had to control the crowds, and from the RTO, the office dealing with the movement of services personnel. Gilbert Matthews then Superintendent of the Line, kindly allowed me to spend some time in this holy of holies, and for several hours I was able to listen to all the various telephone calls, see the messages that were handed in, and to appreciate all the other activities on which a close watch was being kept that morning. The operating department had certainly benefited from the experience of chaotic conditions in the past, and although traffic was heavy on that day the rapid dispositions made never allowed it to reach crisis point, as it had done on some earlier occasions.

The working of empty trains up from the carriage sidings at West London Junction and from Old Oak Common had to be regulated as precisely as the running of scheduled passenger trains on the line; no less so were the light engine movements. The timetabling of the stock movements had to be linked with platform occupancy in Paddington itself, because it would be no use having trains queuing up on the empty carriage line outside. In studying the timetabling of the empty stock movements I had noticed that the empties did not necessarily set out in the same order that the loaded trains would leave and this was due to the platform working. On one holiday weekend the stock for the morning 10.45, 10.55, 11.0 and

11.5 departures from Paddington left Old Oak at 9.20, 9.50, 9.25 and 9.35 – quite out of their eventual sequence. In the Control Coach in No 2 platform at Paddington no fewer than six traffic department men were continuously on duty, each with a telephone at his elbow, closely in touch with every movement the moment it occurred, so that they could immediately be aware of any irregularity and take steps to correct it before it snowballed into a hold-up. While the regular trains running at the same time as at mid-week had a certain proportion of reserved seats the same did not apply to any extent on the many relief trains. Since the Christmas of 1935 the introduction of public address equipment had made crowd control much easier, and I was next to see how they dealt with the loading of the trains.

On every platform as the trains loaded up a check was maintained on the number of passengers travelling, and this was constantly being related to the number observed to be queuing up on the Lawn circulating area. I found my time was fully occupied, because with my locomotive interests there were times when I wanted to be at both ends of Platform 2 at once – to see the engines that were taking the trains out, and to hear the messages constantly arriving in the Control Coach. I saw a beautifully polished *Wardour Castle* back down on to the 14-coach 10.45am to Bristol and Weston-super-Mare; the train itself was no more than an austerity equivalent of the old 11.15am 2-hour express to Bristol. Steps had been taken in the previous autumn to restore it in some way, running non-stop to Bath at an average speed of $55\frac{1}{2}$mph but the drastic order of March 1947 had involved its cancellation, and loading its passengers on to the semi-fast 10.45. Walking back down the platform I saw that it was crowded, and when I got back to the Control Coach a note was just being handed in to advise that it carried 1010 passengers. The 11am substitute for the Cornish Riviera, also loaded to 14-coaches, but although I saw that there were some standing passengers it carried only 800, well below maximum capacity of the stock.

This was good news for Control, because it meant that traffic to the West of England was not unduly heavy, and the likelihood of having to run extra trains later in the day was receding. The loading of that 11am to Penzance was a curious, but characteristic example of crowd psychology. Passengers arriving for the train in the last quarter-hour or so, and finding the rearmost coaches crowded just piled in, to stand in the corridors, whereas if they had walked further forward they would have found many spare seats. The queues out on The Lawn were long, but clearly defined for each prospective departure. There was nothing like that frightful jam of people that congregated on that terrible Saturday when the flying bombs were falling on London, and the Great Western top management was remonstrating with officialdom before authority was given to run even one more train. On the Saturday that I watched from the Control Coach everything was going like clockwork. The 11am to Penzance left two minutes late, from Platform 3, but the shunting engine that brought in the empty stock had barely reached the head end of the platform before the barriers were opened again and passengers for the 11.35am to Carmarthen were surging through. Signalmen in the departure side box were equally on their toes and at 11.8am the stock for the South Wales express was drawn into the same platform from which the Cornish train had so recently left.

I was complimenting one of the senior men in Control on the smoothness with which things were going; but he said, wryly: 'Don't speak too soon. Come back about 5.30 this evening, and you'll see us settling in for a really rough night'. I was surprised at this, because I would have thought by that time the bulk of the holiday traffic would have cleared. But this man directed my attention to what was happening on the arrival side of Paddington station. There was a major sporting event in London that afternoon, and day excursionists from South Wales were arriving in droves. 'We've got to get that lot home tonight', he explained, and the earliest of them were expected to make for the 5.55pm, always a very heavy and popular train without an influx of returning day excursionists. The real crunch began as expected about 5.30pm when the 5.55pm had already become absolutely packed, with passengers lining the corridors throughout; people were sitting on suitcases between the knees of those lucky enough to have ordinary seats. Then the loudspeakers went into action: 'The 5.55pm train for Newport, Cardiff and principal stations to Carmarthen is now loaded to capacity; the next train for South Wales is the 6.55pm'.

By this time however there was real anxiety, because the station police, constantly watching the queuing, reported such a solid phalanx already forming up across the Lawn that there was a doubt if the 6.55pm would be able to clear it. The main part of this train then went through to Fishguard and it included a considerable amount of reserved seat accommodation for Irish boat passengers which was fully booked. Even before the 5.55pm had gone, the barriers leading on to its platform had long since been closed. The 9.25pm to South Wales was already booked to run in two sections, and instructions were sent from the control coach to Old Oak Common to add extra coaches to both, if possible making each to 14-vehicles. The only trouble with the South Wales trains was that if Castle class engines were not available for these maximum loads an assisting engine would be needed for the climb out of the Severn Tunnel, and at times of such pressure one might not be readily available at Pilning, and the line would be blocked while one of these lengthy trains stood waiting for assistance.

Although it is slightly overstepping the limits of this book it must be added that for a few years after nationalisation the passenger situation at holiday weekends became even more acute. Privilege tickets, and the occasional free passes for the staff were no longer confined to the limits of their old railways. They could go anywhere in the British Isles, and many of the north-country railwaymen began to sample the West Country. I well remember talking to the stationmaster and his wife at Kyle of Lochalsh; they had decided to spend their holiday at Penzance, because they added, '. . . it was the farthest they could go'. The Western Region, to protect its regular patrons from being swamped by railwaymen from elsewhere, travelling on passes, or privilege tickets had to place an embargo on the use of such tickets on many of the more popular trains, like the Cornish Riviera, the Torbay, the 3.30pm from Paddington and others, and when I was doing some footplate work and had some appropriate travel facilities I remember having to get a permit to travel on the train at all, because although I should not be occupying a seat, I had to pass through the barrier, and it was one of those trains on which an embargo was placed.

With road haulage still very limited in those first years after the war, and petrol severely rationed, freight traffic on all railways was very heavy, even though output from the coal industry was considerably below overall national requirements. Under the wartime lease-lend arrangements considerable tonnages of coal were being imported from the USA, and as the Great Western, in particular, discovered, it was pretty poor stuff as a locomotive fuel. The situation sunk to the depths of ignominy that some of it was allocated to the GWR for use on the Welsh local lines, and I had one experience of it myself when a 5600 class 0–6–2 tank working a stopping train down the Taff Vale line from Merthyr to Cardiff had to stop several times for the firemen to go down the train releasing the brakes by hand. The engine was steaming so badly that there was not enough steam pressure to keep the vacuum brakes from leaking on. It was this kind of situation that led the Great Western into what was intended to be a limited introduction of oil firing. To lessen the tonnage of coal to be carried for locomotive purposes it was intended to make Cornwall an entirely oil-fired area, while more by way of protest than anything else a number of 2–8–0 freight engines working in South Wales were also equipped. Unfortunately, as is well known, the Government of the day, or rather one particular Ministry working in isolation, seized upon this purely Great Western limited project as an inspiration, and authorised considerable expenditure on the installation of many oil-fuelling plants nationwide. Only when a large amount of public money had been spent did another Government department point out that we had insufficient foreign exchange to purchase the necessary oil!

In those difficult and frustrating years between the end of the war and the onset of nationalisation the Great Western, like the other three major British railways, came in for a good deal of criticism through the comparisons made between pre-war and post-war achievement. While much of this criticism was justified so far as the end product was concerned – such as speed, punctuality and general reliability – those who criticised seemed to have no conception of the changed conditions in which railways were being operated. What was worse, when any attempt was made to enlighten such critics as to what lay behind these deficiences, many of them just did not want to know. The shortfall in performance was used as political capital in favour of nationalisation, and I shall always remember a man of my acquaintance, who I had always respected for the sobriety of his utterance, once remarking that, 'the railways had made such a mess of the job it was time someone else had a go'. He was a man whose wartime travelling had been entirely on the Great Western. Unknown to most of these critics it was not in passenger service, but in freight that the greatest changes of circumstance and the greatest difficulties were arising in 1946–7.

Before the war 'double-home' working, lodging away from home between out and return trips, was a way of life for most established railwaymen, in both passenger and freight service. On the Great Western most of the important express goods trains ran at night, and the working of them was always considered a prestige job for both enginemen and guards. But the war changed all that, and in a way an outsider might not have thought of. It was wrapped up in the one word, housing. During the war not only had the normal house-building programmes of private firms and local authorities been curtailed to the point of complete standstill, but in the larger centres of population vast numbers of houses had been destroyed in the blitz. The shortage of accommodation in such cities as Birmingham, Bristol, Exeter, London and Plymouth was acute enough for the normal residents, without making any provision for train crews on a double-home. Whereas previously the driver, fireman and guard of an express goods train would have gone out as a team knowing that a railwayman's family would provide them a good billet, cook the food they had brought with them, probably giving them reciprocal comforts to what their own menfolk would receive when on similar trips away from home, after the war anyone who had any accommodation beyond family needs had regular boarders. And so, in freight train working the double-home became a thing of the past.

An additional burden was loaded on to Control, and here I mean the permanent Divisional and Headquarters control offices. Arrangements had to be made for re-manning trains at locations where a return working was possible, and train crews could return to their home stations within a single day's duty. The 9.10pm express goods from Paddington to Birkenhead was a case in point. Before the war this train called at Greenford to pick up traffic from Lyons. Then, with a 4700 class 5ft 8in 2–8–0 in charge it ran non-stop from Greenford to Shrewsbury, where the crew booked off and lodged. But when the working was restored after the war, and lodging turns were not to be considered for freight trains, a stop purely for crew-changing was inserted at Banbury South, to enable the London men to return within a single-home duty. In the immediate post-war years this was not always easy. Lines were frequently congested, and even the regular express freights were sometimes running hours behind schedule – sometimes through an engine failure held up for still longer, and combined with a later service having a load far below normal capacity. Then there would come the problem of a crew stranded without a train, and in the middle of the night it would not be easy to find a passenger train in which they could return home as passengers 'on the cushions'. There were indeed many times when the arrangement of enginemen's and guards duties provided Control with as many problems as those of actually running the trains.

In the difficult early months of 1947 when the coal situation was critical, I was able to spend some time in the freight train control office at Reading, which was the principal regulating point in the London traffic division. There the particulars of every train in the area were entered on cards. The details included not only the origin and destination of the train, its loading and the class of engine, but also the duty roster of the enginemen and guard. By this the controller will know at what intermediate station a relief crew must be provided. The relieving of crews, even if a fresh one is ready, takes time. It was a very different matter to that of remanning passenger trains, where, on a station platform it could be done in less than five minutes. With a freight, even if the relief men were waiting in a nearby bothy, by the time the guard had walked up from the end of a long train, and his relief had taken his place one would be lucky to be under way again in much less than half an hour. Furthermore one could not expect the men to take so much interest in a shared activity, probably with another crew who they had never met before, than in one on which they saw the job through from start to finish. The Great Western was fortunate in its own heavy freight engines, of the 28XX class. These were nobly reinforced by the former ROD 2–8–0s of Great Central design, veterans of the first world war, and although so unlike the standard Great Western engines they had been absorbed into the Swindon family and were much appreciated.

In all the control offices a constant check was kept on the movements of all freight engines. The locomotive control officer at Reading, for example, would have been able to say at once how many engines, and of what classes, were on shed at Southall, and how soon each of them would have been ready to take the road. It was a time of acute labour shortage in running sheds, and this reacted upon the daily maintenance situation. Sometimes engines would have been late on to their trains. Control had to keep a continual watch on this, and sometimes the pre-arranged duties were switched so as to minimise delay. Another headache for the freight train control at that time was the number of delays arising from wagon failures. Repair of wagons might seem a relatively minor part of the overall job of running a railway; like everything else in wartime, while not being neglected, the periods between overhauls were strung out far beyond normal. In the days when a high proportion of such wagons were still loose-coupled, the amount of knocking around they received when shunting, or indeed when out on the road, was scarcely believable; and it is astonishing that they withstood such murderous treatment as well as they did. Indeed on many occasions wagons shunted around in marshalling yards were often involved in hefty collisions as rolling wagons hit standing rakes at several miles an hour. Then sooner or later would come the fateful 'stop and examine' bell code on the block telegraph from a signalman who had seen something on a passing freight train that looked wrong. Sometimes it would be nothing worse than a false alarm, but not infrequently in those troubled post-war years, a real danger had been spotted perhaps a broken spring, or hot smoking axlebox. The wagon had to be removed from the train, and consigned to the ranks of the cripples. Another headache for Control! Other traffic was held up while the disabled train was under examination, unless the failure occurred on a four-track section and diversions could be made. The booked roster of the train crew could be upset, and improvisations made necessary, while last but by no means least, arrangements had to be made to transfer the contents of the crippled wagon to another one.

In those far-off days when almost every country station had its goods sidings, and so much traffic was made up of single wagon loads it was very important to have a continuous, and well-nigh up to the minute situation report on all wagons on hand. At each control office throughout the Great Western Railway, a census was taken at 8am of all wagons on hand in traffic department sidings. The results were just becoming available when I was in the control office at Reading, and they came, among others, from Moreton Yard, near Didcot, Maidenhead, Taplow, Slough, Cholsey and Oxford and lower down the scale from stationmasters at local stations with small goods yards. The total in each area was classified according to destination, so that when this daily census was completed, which it was quite early in the day, the controller would have a comprehensive situation report before him. On the day I was there, at Moreton Yard, for example, there were 5 wagons for Abingdon, 27 for High Wycombe, 15 for Poplar, 40 for Paddington, 6 for Denham. Arrangements were already in hand for clearing these wagons, necessarily fitting in any arrangements with the actual number of trains on the line, and determining, for example, which up trains could be put into the yard at Moreton to collect traffic for Paddington or Poplar, and so on. It is indeed a thought-provoking reflection upon the vast changes that have come over railway freight operation in the succeeding 35 years from nationalisation, that the once-extensive yard at Moreton, $1\frac{1}{2}$ miles east of Didcot has now been completely liquidated, and all the siding tracks lifted.

Analysis of the total number of trains on the move was known officially as the 'line position' and in the London Division it was recorded four times a day, with 'news bulletins' passed to the Divisional Superintendent's office at Paddington. The London Division had many complications to contend with, not only in its end-on junctions with other divisions of the GWR but in its contacts with other railways. The flow of freight traffic over these junction points had to be very carefully watched for the reactions that might be set up internally. This applied equally to all other traffic divisions of the railway, but in 1947 it was the London Division and its control office at Reading that came within my particular scrutiny. In Great Western days the London Division had two end-on junctions with the Bristol Division: at Milton signalbox, midway between Didcot and Steventon stations, and at Bedwyn, on the Berks & Hants line. It is interesting to recall how the traffic divisions sometimes differed from the engineering division boundaries, because the latter, between Bristol and London, was half-way between Wantage Road and Challow stations. The London traffic division also had end-on junctions with the Birmingham and with the Worcester Divisions, though neither of these had corresponding engineering divisions. Traffic exchange points with the Southern existed at Reading and Basingstoke so far as the London Division was concerned, as well as at a number of points in the London area. With the LMS there were junctions at Oxford and Acton, as well as on the West London line in the Old Oak – Kensington area, and in all cases a very careful watch had to be kept on incoming traffic.

A headache of an unexpected and unusual kind was provided by a small firm that had a works beside the line near West Drayton, and I was in the Reading control office when the situation erupted. It was of all the more interest to me in that one of the senior executives of that firm was an old colleague of mine who had forsaken railway signal engineering for management on his own account. That morning they reported that their stone crushing plant had broken down, and for the time being they required no stone. The plant was normally in operation continuously for five days in the week, and they took a steady supply from quarries in the South Midlands. At the moment their own private siding was full of loaded wagons of stone, and they had telephoned the GWR to say that they could accept no more until further notice. Reading Control went into immediate action. They knew from the line position and news bulletins how many wagons were on the way. The trains concerned had to be advised, and arrangements made to berth the wagons in some reception yard, like Moreton, and as the traffic originated on the LMS that company had to be advised that no more of this kind could be accepted for the time being. Fortunately however the breakdown at the crushing plant did not appear to be very serious, and the firm advised that they hoped to have it put right in two or three days; accordingly the 'stopper' put on to the LMS was only to hold those wagons that were actually under way. If the portents of hold-up had been more serious the quarries would have been asked not to load any more stone until further notice.

Summer Saturdays, with the peaks of extra passenger traffic can bring their problems, especially where interchange working with other railways was concerned. One particular upheaval, that I well remember, was primarily a crisis for the control staff of the Central and Eastern sections of the Southern, though it came to involve Great Western engines – very much so! At this distance in time I cannot remember what the initial cause of the trouble was, but its effect was to preclude any interchange of Saturday special trains with the Southern's South Eastern line at Reading, although those for the LSW line via Basingstoke could still run. Anything for the Brighton and South Eastern lines had to be taken up the Great Western main line as far as Old Oak Common and then over the West London line. The locomotive situation on the Southern on such days recalled the famous wartime poster 'There isn't even half an engine to spare' without the incidence of crises over interchange traffic, and on this particularly busy Saturday the engines that were waiting to take Kent Coast trains from the Great Western at Reading could not be used. Trains from all parts began to queue up at Addison Road (today's Kensington Olympia). The Southern locomotive control did wonders of improvisation, by extending enginemen's duty hours, enrolling readily forthcoming volunteers. But there was a limit, and then Authority had an idea: certain trains which would normally have diverged at Reading and travelled via Guildford would have fresh engines waiting for them at Redhill, where engines would be changed in any case. Why not let the Great Western engines which had brought them to Addison Road continue down the Brighton line. There was a train waiting still with its GW engine coupled; there was a Southern man ready to go as conductor, the GW men also were willing, but what about the engine? The Southern supervisor at Stewarts Lane asked its number: 53XX came the reply. A GWR Mogul was all right so far as route availability was concerned, and the supervisor gave his consent, immediately becoming further immersed in a welter of engine-finding and manning problems. The train with the Great Western engine, and the Southern pilotman found its way down the Brighton main line, and duly uncoupled at Redhill, to the consternation of the local foreman, for the engine was not a 53XX but a 59XX – a Hall class 4–6–0, just that much wider across the cylinders and steps to be outside the SR's structure gauge! It must have only just cleared the platform edges on the way. Having got there it was not allowed to move out again. I never heard how the Great Western got its engine back, because all routes to its native land were officially barred to it. Nevertheless it was not the last occasion that a Hall got to Redhill.

Another instance, this time of Great Western men acting on their own initiative *without* reference to any form of higher authority had an amusing sequel, all the more so in the way it showed how the Great Western tradition lingered into post-nationalisation days. It happened on the very steep ascent out of Weymouth, leading to Bincombe Tunnel, where the gradient is 1 in 50 for two miles. One of the Southern West Country class Pacifics hauling the three-coach Weymouth portion of the Royal Wessex express, characteristically, started slipping on the steep gradient, and once into Bincombe Tunnel, on 1 in 52, it not only stalled but slithered out backwards; the rearmost bogie of the last coach went through a pair of catch points into one of those lengthy sand drags. The train thereupon became completely stuck! The fireman walked through the tunnel to the signalbox at the north end to report their plight, and thereupon the local men of the Great Western, without any prompting, reference to Control or anyone else, mounted an astonishing rescue operation.

The Bincombe Tunnel signalman telephoned Dorchester. The stationmaster there had a Hall class engine on hand, and after a quick word with its crew they uncoupled from their train, and armed with a wrong-line order went off tender first to Bincombe.

Feeling their way cautiously down through the tunnel they coupled on to the Bulleid Pacific. But even the efforts of a sure-footed Hall, and a less sure-footed WC could not move that train, with its rear wheels in the sand-drag. Back went the Southern fireman to report the position and to suggest that Bournemouth should be advised not to keep the main part of 'The Royal Wessex' waiting for its Weymouth portion, because they looked like being very late. Meanwhile a down Great Western goods train had arrived at Dorchester, with a Grange 4–6–0 in charge. The state of emergency over-rode all other considerations, and the stationmaster enlisted their aid. They, too uncoupled from their train, and went wrong line to Bincombe. So, the two Great Western 4–6–0s succeeded in lifting the apparently impotent Bulleid 4–6–2 and its three-coach train out of its misery, and having brought it into Dorchester saw it on its way. The cream of the story came next day when the Southern rang up the Bristol Divisional Superintendent to thank him for his assistance, and it was the first the latter officer had heard of it! The Great Western Stationmaster at Dorchester GW, having cleared the obstruction, never thought to report the incident to his boss.

137

11
Special trains and 'Trip'

Some railways in the pre-grouping age, and to some extent after it, regarded the running of trains outside the regularly scheduled timetable service as a nuisance. At one time certain companies in the 19th century deplored the introduction of Bank Holidays, because far from the likelihood of any extra traffic being created they would interfere with the ordinary service. From the beginning of the 20th century at any rate this was never an attitude of the Great Western; in fact certain special train workings were considered to be of such importance as to claim priority over regular trains. Thoughts naturally go back to the Ocean Mail specials that were the subject of such close attention and magnificent locomotive work in the early 1900s, until the terrible accident in 1906 on the London & South Western Railway at Salisbury put an end to the highly competitive nature of this particular activity. Even so the working of the mail trains remained a highly important traffic, so much so that mail vans with slip apparatus were built so that the main train could be run non-stop from Plymouth Millbay docks to Paddington, detaching the vans containing the North Country mails by slipping at Bedminster. Churchward's new express locomotives were allocated to these trains, even though the load from Bedminster to Paddington, via the Bristol avoiding line, was often no more than two large vans.

At Plymouth the incoming ocean mail traffic came principally from the North German liners, but in West Wales the big development at the port of Fishguard showed Great Western ambitions to be aiming far beyond the regular packet services across St George's Channel, to Rosslare. With the great British steamship lines Cunard and White Star sailing from Liverpool, the London & North Western Railway had hitherto enjoyed the cream of the North American ocean traffic, and the association was close enough for a famous class of 19th century Crewe locomotives to have nine out of its ten members named after White Star liners. But it needs no more than a glance at a map of the British Isles to show the advantage of Fishguard as a port of call for inward-bound liners from the USA. While there was no question of the great Cunarders and White Star liners *docking* at Fishguard, if passengers for London, and indeed for destinations on the continent of Europe were set down by tender at Fishguard a whole day could be saved on the journey from New York, obviating the continuing sea passage and the necessarily slow, and often much delayed arrival in the Mersey.

Monday 30 August 1909 was a memorable day in Great Western history, for on that morning the *Mauretania*, eastbound from New York, made her first call at Fishguard. The occasion had much of the pomp and circumstance of a royal train. So many passengers were expected to avail themselves of this new facility that no fewer than three special trains were provided, the first taking the mails, the second and third, made up to 10 and 11 vehicles respectively conveying the passengers and their luggage. All three made only one stop between Fishguard and Paddington, at Cardiff to change engines. As indicating the kind of patronage expected seating in the two trains provided for 288 first, and only 112 third class passengers. Both trains had lavish restaurant car accommodation. On the day in question all ordinary traffic at Fishguard was completely suspended between 10am and 4pm, while the special instruction notice issued to all concerned with the running of these trains said: 'It is of supreme importance that an ABSOLUTELY clear road be kept for each of the special trains'. One can indeed wonder to what extent the ordinary service was interrupted by such an imperious order, extending over the entire $261\frac{1}{2}$ miles from Fishguard Harbour to Paddington, because it was not that a carefully planned timetable path had been arranged beforehand – just that the specials should be worked through in five hours overall, or less.

The importance attached to the occasion seems barely believable in these days, when rapid travel between England and the USA is the experience of countless thousands. But in 1909 it was sufficient for the GWR Assistant Superintendent of the Line, Charles Aldington (afterwards General Manager), and J. B. Morris of the Publicity Department, to cross the Atlantic in order to travel back in the *Mauretania*, while the Chairman himself, Viscount Churchill, went across to Ireland to join the liner when she called to set down passengers by tender at Queenstown (now Cobh). To set the seal on all the arrangements at Fishguard itself, Sir James Inglis, the General Manager, and several other senior officers had been in residence for several days beforehand. But in one respect there was uncertainty until the very last minute. They had no idea previously as to what time the *Mauretania* would arrive.

The harbour station, snugly ensconced on a rocky hillside, has no sight of the open sea, and a look-out post with a field telephone had to be set up on a headland, so that the station and all concerned could be alerted the moment the great liner was sighted, far out at sea. Then, three Great Western tenders put out to meet her, one for the mails, one for the passengers, and one for their luggage. All three trains were hauled from Fishguard to Cardiff by 4–4–0 engines of the Churchward inside cylinder type. An Atbara, the *Maine*, had the three-coach mail; a City and a Flower the *Halifax* and the *Gardenia*, had the first passenger special, with *Anemone* and *Mignonette*, both Flowers on the second. The times of the three trains over the 116.2 miles from Fishguard to Cardiff were 127, 131 and 136½ minutes. The working of the second and third trains, even with two engines, involved no mean feats of locomotive performance, not so much in power output as in ekeing out the water supply. With only one set of troughs intermediately, at Ferryside, roughly 50 miles from the start, considerable ingenuity must have been exercised to enable both engines on a double-headed train to get a fill-up. G. A. Sekon, the Founder Editor of *The Railway Magazine*, was a passenger on the first of the two trains, and he reported that water was picked up at practically full speed. From Cardiff all three trains were taken forward by brand new four-cylinder 4–6–0s of the series of Stars named after Kings.

It was as much in anticipation of still faster and more competitive running with these Ocean specials as in avoiding the traffic congestion and severe gradients of the Swansea area that the Swansea District Lines were constructed, and brought into service in July 1913. The new main line was 17 miles long beginning at Court Sart Junction, about mid-way between Briton Ferry and Neath, rejoining the old line at Llandilo Junction East, just before Llanelly. Its great merit was in having no gradient steeper than 1 in 120, compared to the frightful banks between Neath and Gowerton, and also in having no more than a few moderate speed restrictions. This was not all, so far as Great Western aspirations towards the Ocean traffic at Fishguard were concerned. In July

1914 it obtained an Act authorising construction of an extension to the Swansea District Line, from Morlais Junction to Pembrey, by-passing Llanelly, and its freight traffic complications, and providing a further 10 miles of fine open road. Even before these new lines were completed, non-stop running between Fishguard and Paddington had been contemplated with the Ocean specials, and Star class 4–6–0 engines were working into Fishguard. But of course the outbreak of war in August 1914 halted any plans for implementing the provisions of the Act, and after the war the transfer of both Cunard and White Star activities from Liverpool to Southampton ended any hopes of reviving activity at Fishguard as an Ocean liner port.

The redeployment of Transatlantic steamship services however gave the Great Western a new field for its enterprise in running special boat trains. Both Cunard and the White Star lines in the years immediately after the war were called upon to handle a large volume of traffic to and from the Continent, which previously had been carried by German liners. The magnificient Hamburg–America ship *Imperator* had been handed over to Cunard in replacement for the torpedoed *Lusitania*; renamed the *Berengaria* she joined the *Mauretania* and *Aquitania* in maintaining the express service to New York. For the convenience of the large number of passengers for the Continent the big liners called first at Cherbourg before crossing the Channel and berthing at Southampton, and the Great Western saw an excellent way of cashing in on this situation by inducing the eastbound liners to call briefly at Plymouth, and set down passengers and mails by tender. In this way passengers from New York to London would save a day, and incidentally bring some prestige traffic to the Great Western that would otherwise have gone to the Southern between Southampton and Waterloo! When the liners did call all concerned on the GWR saw to it that the boat trains got a fast and undelayed run from Millbay Docks to Paddington. While the Cornish Riviera Express was restored to its pre-war schedule of 4hr 7min non-stop from Paddington to Plymouth (North Road) the boat trains were expected to cover the longer distance up from Millbay Docks in the level four hours, but were generally considerably lighter trains than the down Limited.

Before the war the *Mauretania* and the *Lusitania* were the speed champions of the North Atlantic, and soon after the service was resumed in all its old splendour the *Mauretania* began distinguishing herself by breaking her own pre-war records for the eastbound crossing. In the autumn of 1924 she made a new record of 4 days 21 hours 57 minutes from New York to Plymouth, which the GWR fitly rounded off by working the boat train from Millbay to Paddington in 3hr 56min, an average speed of 57.6mph. The train conveyed 100 passengers, and consisted of five coaches, including restaurant car, and two of the large Ocean Mail stowage vans for mails. It was hauled by a Castle class locomotive. Leaving Plymouth at 6.33pm it was not difficult to provide a clear road, but that was not always the case with special trains run in connection with liners other than those of Cunard. The new German liner *Bremen*, in 1929, was taking up the challenge for the Blue Riband of the Atlantic crossing, and the boat train run in connection from Plymouth was in a fair way to making a new record for the run to Paddington, when an operating error at Westbury resulted in a loss of about 10 minutes. Even so, the seven-coach train, hauled by *Queen Alexandra*, then rebuilt to the Castle class, reached Paddington in 238 minutes, inclusive of two other slight checks. The net average speed from Millbay Docks, including the necessarily very slow start, was over 60mph throughout.

The grandest occasion of boat train special working from Plymouth came on 15 March 1937 when the new giant Cunard White Star liner *Queen Mary* made her first call. It was a civic as well as a transport occasion, with the Mayor of Plymouth according an appropriate welcome to the liner; so many passengers availed themselves of the faster journey to London, than by staying on the ship until she docked at Southampton, that two special trains loaded to no less than 326 and 412 tons were necessary. With Castle class engines, both needed double-heading over the South Devon line, but despite the need to stop at Newton Abbot West, to set down the pilot engines – in each case of the 4–4–0 Bulldog type – the overall times from passing Plymouth North Road (about five minutes running time from the docks) to arrival in Paddington were 3hr 46min and 4hr exactly, while the start-to-stop average speeds over the 193.7 miles from Newton Abbot were $63\frac{1}{2}$ and $60\frac{1}{2}$mph. For the record, the two makers of these very fine runs were *Montgomery Castle* and *Tintagel Castle*.

Turning now to another kind of special train, I have emphasised previously in this book how the Great Western set store in its close association with the life, business and pleasures of the country it served. This was in no respect more so than in its provision for special trains in connection with important race meetings. Generally speaking many of the express train services to and from London were worked by engines and men from the country sheds, the West of England turns from Plymouth and Newton Abbot being no exception; but the Cheltenham Flyer was always an Old Oak job, for the simple reason that it ensured keeping plenty of London drivers familiar with the road to Gloucester regularly, and Cheltenham occasionally. Race traffic for the Cheltenham meetings was also considered a priority, and it was necessary to maintain a link of drivers who could work the specials. The Cheltenham race meetings were always regarded, unofficially, as a social occasion for senior Great Western officers, who foregathered there whether they had racing interest or not; one can imagine the consternation and carefully veiled fury that prevailed when, in BR days, the iconoclastic Stanley Raymond called a meeting of senior executive officers at Paddington on Cheltenham Gold Cup day!

Traffic to Newbury on race days also received preferential treatment. For some reason that I cannot remember now I chose to make one of my periodic visits from Bath to London via Westbury, joining the up Dutchman there, for what I expected to be a non-stop run to Paddington. When the train arrived from the west it was much heavier than I anticipated: 15 coaches, crowded with passengers, and amounting to at least 535 tons behind the tender. But the engine, No 6010 *King Charles I*, and its crew were in top form, and despite very bad weather the climb to Savernake was most competently made. Then, to my surprise, we stopped at Newbury Racecourse station, to set down a large number of race goers. I thought it remarkable that so important an express should have been stopped to favour excursionists, not only so, but worked so vigorously as to lose no time through making the extra stop. It is true that then, in 1950, the schedule allowed 116 minutes for the 95.6 miles from Westbury to Paddington. But in addition to the extra stop at Newbury Racecourse we had other delays, totalling 14 minutes in running time. Despite this we were exactly on time arriving in Paddington, having given racegoers from the West Country the luxury of a ride in this crack express.

The Newbury specials from Paddington, usually booked to run the 52 miles to the Racecourse station in 62 minutes, were treated as priority traffic. The timing of the Members and First Class only train, leaving Paddington at 11.50am meant essentially that there should be no dallying on the way. Immediately behind it was the

Head Code ..	B	B	A	B	A	A	A	A	A
DOWN.	8.10 a.m. Reading to Bristol.	7.45 a.m. Slough Diesel.	8.15 a.m. Paddington Staff Train.	9.43 a.m. Reading to Westbury.	10.25 a.m. Reading Diesel.	Tote and Passenger Special.	Ordinary Train.	11.35 a.m. Reading to Trowbridge.	Paddington Special.
	a.m.	a.m.		a.m.	a.m.	a.m.	a.m.	a.m.	a.m.
PADDINGTON dep.	..	..		..	..	10 13 ML	10 30 ML	..	11 25 ML
Old Oak Common ,,	..	..		..	..			..	B
Ealing ,,	..	..		..	..	10 24		..	
Southall ,,	..	..		..	..	10 30	10 43	..	11 38
Slough ,,	..	..		..	..	10 39	10 52	..	11 47 B
Maidenhead ,,	..	..		..	..	10 45	10 58½	..	11 53
READING { arr.						10 58	11 11	..	12 5
READING { dep.	8 10	8 26	*(Empty Coaches of this train to work through to Newbury Town. See page.)*	9 43	10 25	..	..	11 35	..
Reading West Jct. ,,	G	G		G	G	..	..	S	..
Oxford Road Jct. ,,						—	—	—	—
Reading West Stn. ,,	8 13	8 29		9 47		—	—	—	—
Theale ,,	8 21½	8 37		9 55	10 34½	—	—	—	—
Aldermaston ,,	8 29½	8 44½		10 2	10 41	—	—	—	—
Midgham ,,	8 34½	8 48½		10 7	10 45	—	—	—	—
Thatcham ,,	8 41	8 55		10 13	10 51	—	—	—	—
NEWBURY { arr.	8 46	9 0		10 18	10 56	11 18	..	11 56	12 25
(Race Course) { dep.	8 47	9 1		10 19	10 57	..	..	11 57	12¼28
NEWBURY { arr.	8 49	9 3		10 21	10 59	..	11 29½	11 59	12¼30
(Town Stn.) { dep.	8 50	..		10 36	..	..	..	12 0	..
Platform at R.C. Station	1	3	..	1	3	1	..	1	..
Empty Trains to run to or start from						Race Course Siding. No. 5.			N'bury Town No. 2 Loop.

B—11.20 a.m. Paddington to run RL throughout.   G—To call specially at **Newbury Race Course.** Reading and **Thatcham** to instruct Trainmen.   S—To call specially at **Newbury Race Course.** Reading to instruct Trainmen.

Head Code ..	A	A	A	A	A	B	A
DOWN	Acton Special.	Paddington Special.	Paddington Special. Members' and First Class.	Ordinary Train.	Paddington Special.	12.43 p.m. Reading Ordinary Retimed.	Ordinary Train.
	a.m.	a.m.	a.m.	noon	p.m.	p.m.	p.m.
PADDINGTON dep.	Z RL	11 40 ML	11 50 ML	12 0 ML	12 5 ML	..	12 30 ML
Old Oak Common ,,	9¼25	—	—	—	A	..	—
Acton ,,	11 7					..	
Ealing ,,							12 43
Southall ,,		11 53	12 3	12 13	12 18		12 52
Slough ,,		12 2	12 12	12 22	12 27		12 58
Maidenhead ,,		12 20	12 18	12 28	12 33		1 13
READING { arr.							
READING { dep.	*(For complete times and calling Stations, see page.)*	—	—	12 40	12 45	12 48 G	1S18
Reading West Jct. ,,		—	—			G	..
Oxford Road Jct. ,,		—	—			—	—
Reading West Stn. ,,		—	—	—	—	12 51	—
Theale ,,		—	—	—	—	12 59	—
Aldermaston ,,		—	—	—	—	1 6	—
Midgham ,,		—	—	—	—	1 11	—
Thatcham ,,		—	—	—	—	1 17	—
NEWBURY { arr.	12 35	12 40	12 50	—	1 5	1 22	1 39
(Race Course) { dep.	12¼37	..	..	..	..	1 23	1 40
NEWBURY { arr.	12¼39	..	..	12 58½	..	1 25	1 42
(Town Stn.) { dep.	..	..	..	..	..	1 52	1 45
Platform at R.C. Station	3	1	1	..	1	3	1
Empty Trains to run to or start from	Newbury Town No. 1 Loop.	Race Course Siding No. 1.	Race Course Siding No. 4.	*Amended times.*	—	Stable in No. 2 Platform.	—

A—10.35 a.m. Kensington Milk Empties to be kept clear.   G—To call specially at **Newbury Race Course.** Reading and **Thatcham** to instruct Trainmen.   S—To call specially at **Newbury Race Course.** Reading to instruct Trainmen.
Z—Empty Coaches from West London.

FRIDAY and SATURDAY, 22nd and 23rd OCTOBER—continued.

FORMATION OF PADDINGTON SPECIALS.

10.13 a.m. Paddington Tote Special. (No. 4 Line **ML.**)

Brake Compo, Compo, 3 Thirds, Compo, Brake Compo, Brake Compo, 3 Thirds, Brake Compo (Corridor Stock). (The leading seven vehicles will form 3.50 p.m. Return Special.)

11.25 a.m. Paddington Special (No. 4 Line **ML**).

Van Third **X**, 2 Firsts (non-corridor), 3 Thirds **X**, 2 Compos **X**, 3 Thirds **X**, Van Third **X**.

11.40 a.m. Paddington Special. (No. 5 Line **ML.**)

Van Third **X**, 2 Firsts (non-corridor), 3 Thirds **X**, 2 Compos **X**, 3 Thirds **X**, Van Third **X**.

11.50 p.m. Paddington (Members and First Class). (No. 4 Line **ML.**)

Brake First (6 compartments—with tables), **First Dining Saloon, Kitchen Car, First Dining Saloon, First** (8 compartments with 2 toilets), **Dining Car, 2 Firsts, Kitchen First** (Kitchen end trailing), **First Dining Saloon, 2 Firsts, Brake First** (6 compartments).

12. 5 p.m. Paddington Special. (No. 5 Line **ML.**)

Brake First, 2 Firsts (8 compartments), Kitchen First (Kitchen End trailing), Vestibule 3rd, 6 Thirds, Van Third (Corridor Stock).

PLATFORMS AT NEWBURY RACE COURSE STATION AT WHICH THE SPECIAL TRAINS WILL ARRIVE AND DEPART.

From	Due at	Plat-form No.	Disposal of Empty Train.	Return Empty Train to leave for Race Course Station.	Forms Return Train from Race Course at	Plat-form No.
	a.m.			p.m.	p.m.	
Paddington (Passenger and Tote Special)	11 18	1	Race Course Siding .. {	—	3 50	1
	p.m.			—	5 20	1
Wolverhampton J	12 14	2	Race Course Down Loop¶¶	—	4 33	1
Paddington	12 25	1	Newbury Town No. 2 Loop	4†21	4 35	2
Acton..	12 35	3	Newbury Town No. 1 Loop	4†32	4 40	4
Paddington	12 40	1	Race Course Siding ..	—	4 25	1
Paddington (Members and First Class)	12 50	1	**Race Course Siding**	—	4 15	1
Cardiff	1 2	4	Newbury Race Course Up Loop¶	—	4 42	3
Paddington	1 5	2	Stable in No. 2 Platform	—	4 20	2

J—From Oxford on Friday, 22nd October.

¶—For subsequent transfer to Newbury Race Course Down Loop.

¶¶—For subsequent transfer to No. 2 Siding, Newbury Race Course.

11.55 to South Wales, followed by the Torbay Express, due to pass Newbury, one mile beyond the Racecourse station, at 12.58. My great friend D. S. M. Barrie, who later became Chairman and General Manager of the Eastern Region of British Railways, was a passenger on the 11.50 one day and logged a performance that could well stand on a pedestal among special train runs on the Western. The train was made up to 13 coaches, equal to a full load of 465 tons, and the engine as usual a superbly polished up King, No 6025 *King Henry III*. Two severe permanent way speed restrictions were in force, one on each side of Slough station, the effect of which could be crippling for timekeeping; and with such a close succession of trains the reaction back on to later ones could be serious. But all concerned determined that whatever other trains were doing reaction from the 11.50am race special should be minimal.

The start out of Paddington was extremely vigorous, with speed worked up to 72mph before the first permanent way slowing; and at the second one the train was practically stopped, down to no more than 3mph at Farnham Royal box. But then came a quite fantastic acceleration, and on the long very slight rise from Maidenhead to Twyford speed was pounded up to no less than $77\frac{1}{2}$mph. This would have involved an output of 1400 horsepower at the drawbar, which was considerably more than the maxima registered in the all-out trials of No 6001 in 1953. Never in the distinguished history of the Cornish Riviera Express have I seen such an effort here with a comparable load. According to Swindon reckoning it was more than the boiler could sustain continuously; but of course there was a respite to come, while the train was running with steam shut off through the junctions at Reading. Once on to the Berks & Hants line however the men on *King Henry III* tore into it again, and on the markedly rising gradients up the Kennet Valley the exceptional speed of 68mph was reached at Aldermaston; despite those two very bad checks at Slough, which cost about six minutes between them, the special stopped at Newbury Racecourse in exactly one hour from Paddington, two minutes early! In sending me these details Barrie wrote that as far as he was concerned this was the best and most thrilling race of the day. As an aside, the Members' train and one or two other race specials to Newbury usually included lunch prepared in two full kitchen cars; as it had to be served, eaten, and paid for in the bare hour the crews had to work fast.

One could not be long in Swindon in the early spring, whether in the locomotive or carriage works, in the station buffets, or anywhere in the town itself for that matter, without overhearing some talk about 'Trip'. It was obviously something that deeply concerned not only railway workers and their families but the entire community, and that of the surrounding villages also. Greatly intrigued, and having many friends both in the railway service and outside it one makes a few discreet enquiries to find that it was a great annual occasion, the origin of which goes back almost to the dawn of Great Western history. From its inception the Company had a high regard for the welfare of its staff and workforce, and when Gooch decided upon Swindon for the establishment of the locomotive works it was not the Swindon mentioned in Domesday Book, the 'town on the hill', but a location down in the valley below, at the junction with the Gloucester branch, which when Brunel went to look at it and confirmed Gooch's recommendation was 'then only green fields'. Although it was not until February 1841 that the Board authorised the construction of the works, by 1844 the Mechanics Institution had been established 'for the purpose of disseminating useful knowledge and encouraging rational amusement amongst all classes of people employed by the Great Western Railway'. Gooch was the first president, and Brunel was made an honorary member. Its name was later changed to the Mechanics Institute.

Membership of the Institute was actively encouraged by the Great Western Railway, and its rapidly extending educational and recreational facilities were strongly backed by the Company. Then, as a further inducement to join, one free pass a year to anywhere on the system was granted to all members. At the start, when the initial membership under Gooch's presidency was only 15 this did not present any major problems when the day excursion was taken; but as the Works grew and membership increased rapidly it became something that needed careful organisation. Naturally the workmen could only exercise their annual free pass during the week in which the works was closed, and this brought complications. At the time of its maximum activity the locomotive, carriage and wagon works employed about 14,000 people, all of whom naturally belonged to the Mechanics Institute, to secure that travel facility; and when one added wives and families, who would also be involved, a high proportion of the total population of Swindon, then about 60,000, was accounted for. The whole affair became known as Trip, whether that prized pass was exercised as no more

147

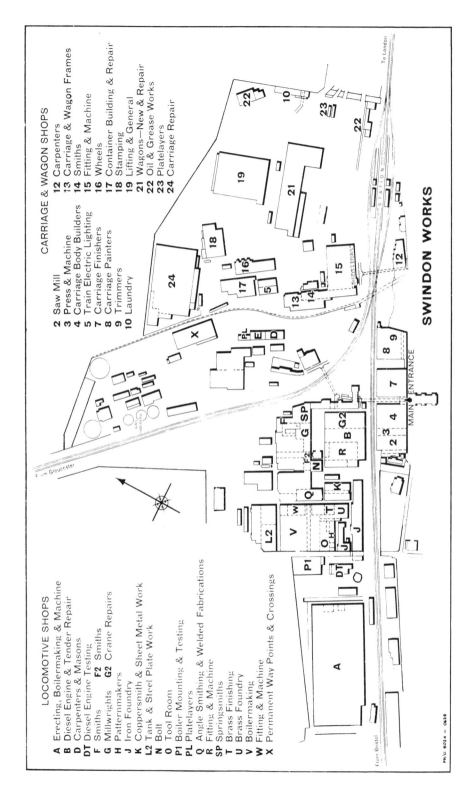

LOCOMOTIVE SHOPS

- **A** Erecting, Boilermaking & Machine
- **B** Diesel Engine & Tender Repair
- **D** Carpenters & Masons
- **DT** Diesel Engine Testing
- **F** Smiths **F2** Smiths
- **G** Millwrights **G2** Crane Repairs
- **H** Patternmakers
- **J** Iron Foundry
- **K** Coppersmith & Sheet Metal Work
- **L2** Tank & Steel Plate Work
- **N** Bolt
- **O** Tool Room
- **P1** Boiler Mounting & Testing
- **PL** Platelayers
- **Q** Angle Smithing & Welded Fabrications
- **R** Fitting & Machine
- **SP** Springsmiths
- **T** Brass Finishing
- **U** Brass Foundry
- **V** Boilermaking
- **W** Fitting & Machine
- **X** Permanent Way Points & Crossings

CARRIAGE & WAGON SHOPS

- **2** Saw Mill
- **3** Press & Machine
- **4** Carriage Body Builders
- **5** Train Electric Lighting
- **7** Carriage Finishers
- **8** Carriage Painters
- **9** Trimmers
- **10** Laundry
- **12** Carpenters
- **13** Carriage & Wagon Frames
- **14** Smiths
- **15** Fitting & Machine
- **16** Wheels
- **17** Container Building & Repair
- **18** Stamping
- **19** Lifting & General
- **21** Wagons—New & Repair
- **22** Oil & Grease Works
- **23** Platelayers
- **24** Carriage Repair

SWINDON WORKS

PR/o 5024 — 0639

than a day excursion to the seaside, or for a longer stay. Trip became as much part of the civic calendar in Swindon as for those 'inside' as the GWR workforce was always euphemistically described in the town.

So, over the years, Trip developed into the most extensive, complex and highly organised movement of railway excursionists that this country has ever seen. Preparations for it, believe it or not, began soon after Christmas each year, although the week during which the works closed did not come until early July. The Mechanics Institute began activities early in the New Year, with a very comprehensive display, in the Reading Room, of brochures from every holiday resort served by the GWR. Perusal of these, and discussion was endless, and for a time in Swindon it seemed that the one topic of conversation was 'Where are you going Trip?' It was never 'the' Trip, 'your' Trip or any other embellishment; just 'Trip'. By April it had been found from previous years' experience that the majority had made up their minds where to go, and for how long within the week, and members went to the Institute on set days for the examination of their membership cards. If they were found in order they were stamped and dated. In these more critical days this would probably have been regarded as a piece of unnecessary officialdom. The modest subscription was no more than fourpence a week, and this covered *all* the member's family as well as the breadwinner himself, and it was in any case deducted from his weekly pay packet. In those days no one minded the check-up. It all formed part of the eager anticipation of Trip.

The town joined wholeheartedly in the preparations; there were 'Trip Shopping Weeks', in which wives and daughters of those 'inside' joined with the utmost enthusiasm. But the real business from the railway point of view came towards the end of May when members had to report to the Institute where they had decided to go. The solicitude with which the well-being of the staff was regarded by the GWR was shown in their being no restriction so far as members of a family was concerned. They were not required to go to the same resort, or on the same day; but all those entitled to passes had to make up their minds beforehand, and adhere to it afterwards. There could be no changes of heart at the last minute. Destination for any of the family on a member's card could be anywhere from Penzance to Pwllheli; from Weston-super-Mare to Weymouth. One British holiday tradition, however, was denied to Trip; there could be no Saturday to Saturday bookings. The traffic department of the GWR insisted that it must not be at a weekend, and must in any case be over and done with well before the peak period of the August Bank Holiday. Accordingly the works closed down at midday on a Thursday.

Although Trip involved the conveyance of some 30,000 people from Swindon in a very short time, in one quite vital respect the Traffic Department had one tremendous advantage in providing for it. Unlike other holiday occasions when they were dealing with the general public, and never knew with any certainty how many people were going to turn up at major stations, and expect to be carried to X, Y or Z, with Trip the Mechanics Institute could provide, well in advance, the exact number of passengers requiring to be taken to South Devon, Cornwall, or even for stations beyond GWR territory such as Blackpool. The Traffic Department organisation worked like clockwork. This enormous exodus from the town took place between 8.30pm on the Thursday evening and 7.7am on the Friday morning. Vast quantities of additional rolling stock had to be collected at Swindon, and to avoid interference with the regular passenger trains, many of the Trip excursions did not leave from either of the two ordinary passenger stations Swindon had in those days. The GWR station on the main line was Swindon Junction; the other one, Swindon Town, was on the Midland & South Western Junction line that ran from Cheltenham to its junction with the West of England main line of the Southern at Andover. As Trip week approached, the Rodbourne Lane Sawmills sidings became filled with excursion trains marshalled up ready, while in the Carriage Works sidings, a similar assembly was taking place. When each man collected his pass for himself and his family from the Mechanics Institute, about a week before the actual holiday week he was given particulars of the train by which he must travel, or if he had chosen a resort to which the numbers did not justify a special train, information as to the regular train, and of the place, or places where he must change.

I have often thought that railway journalists have missed the opportunity of a lifetime in not seeking permission to witness the departure of 30,000 of the denizens of Swindon for their annual holiday in the $10\frac{1}{2}$ hours between 8.30pm on the Thursday and 7am the following morning. The first train away was the 8.30pm for Penzance, first stop Newton Abbot, and that stop in all probability was only to attach an assisting engine for the heavy gradients of the South Devon line. Six more trains left Swindon Junction station between that first departure and 11.45pm. Until then there had been a well-nigh ceaseless trek towards the station; and there, care had to be taken to see that the Trip excursionists did not get into the regular express to South Wales that left at 11.25pm with sleeping cars for Neyland, nor into the Aberdeen–Penzance through service, which arrived from the north at 11.32pm and which was attached to the 9.50pm sleeper from Paddington, which left at midnight. The trek recommenced at 4am on the Friday morning, with the first train away leaving Rodbourne Lane carriage sidings at 4.55am. There was then a difference in the manner of the organisation. The overnight trains, all despatched from the station, were handled as normal passenger excursion trains by the Traffic Department; but in the early morning on the Friday it was a Works job. Passengers had to be admitted to Works property, provision made for them to climb from the six-foot into the carriages, and careful arrangements made to see that no one got into the wrong train. After all, trains were following each other down the line at less than 10 minute intervals for about two hours.

K. J. Cook, who was Locomotive Works Manager for so many years, and in later years Chief Mechanical & Electrical Engineer of the Eastern Region of British Railways, tells a good story about a young lady who nearly missed her train. One might have thought that with the Works shut down on Thursday noon for Trip a senior executive officer would have been ready to relax for a while; but as for many of his fellow officers, for Cook the Great Western Railway was the breath of life, and he felt it was no more than a gesture of appreciation for 50 weeks of good service for the Boss to come down to the Works sidings to see them off on Trip morning, and he was usually down there by 4.30am. One such day, that he recalled with a relish, one of the last of the procession, the 6.50am to Taunton, was ready to pull out of Rodbourne Lane sawmill sidings when a man that he knew put his head out of a carriage window just as the guard was giving the right away and shouted that his daughter was only just coming along. Cook shouted back that he would put her on the 7.05am to Weston-super-Mare, the very last of the specials, and at that moment the 6.50 began to move. The man shouted back that it was no good, because they were going to Burnham-on-Sea, must change at Highbridge and that the Weston-super-Mare train did not go that far.

Cook, walking quickly beside the moving train told him to pull the communication cord, but the man, a long established railwayman hesitated, having visions of the £5 penalty; but Cook persisted 'Go on, pull it!'; he did, and the train began to grind to a halt. Meanwhile the girl had arrived, and as she was being hustled unceremoniously on to the train, the brake valve on the end of the coach had opened when the man pulled the communication cord, and let air into the vacuum brake system. But having got the girl on board Cook climbed up to the coach end, reset the valve, and jumped down again, to see an anxious fireman looking back from the 43XX class 2–6–0 engine, evidently wondering why the brakes were dragging! They had 13 on, anyway. But then the brakes came off, and as Cook remarked: '. . . away they went, no one else any the wiser'! It was a delightfully impromptu and successful way of bending the rules of railway operation, fully in the spirit of Trip; but even in the fullest flowering of the Great Western tradition, when senior officers had a fatherly feeling towards their staffs, I cannot imagine that many of them would have acted thus.

Trip had an influence on affairs in Swindon far beyond the running of trains, and was a remarkable example of community life in one of the old railway towns. In the early spring of 1934 the Graduates Section of the Institution of Mechanical Engineers arranged a Saturday visit to Swindon for its London members. It was to be a varied day beginning, as soon as we arrived by the 9.15am from Paddington, with a visit to the Garrard Engineering Company, which had been established in Swindon during the first world war, and manufactured some of the lightest of mechanical engineering products, such as gramophone motors, automatic record changers and such like. It was an excellent firm and its products a striking contrast to the heavy engineering we were to see in the Locomotive Works later in the day. The minuteness of the component parts greatly interested a couple of young pupils from Ashford who were my companions for the day. It was ideal work for female labour, and of that there is a good story to be told of the overriding influence of Trip in Swindon affairs. In 1919 when normal conditions for holidays were being re-established after the war Garrards fixed the annual holiday for the first week in August. Many of the employees were daughters of men who were 'inside', and a spokesman for them went to the Managing Director of Garrards and pointed out that Trip was early in July. That cut no ice with him until many of his workpeople with Great Western free passes in their pockets were away for Trip week, *and* Garrard's own holiday. In subsequent years the holiday weeks were the same!

Even before the steam era ended, and the running down of Swindon Works began the old traditions surrounding Trip had begun to disappear. After the second world war and the overwhelming victory of Labour in the General Election of 1945, trades union interests and influence in the Works became stronger, and the Works Committee took exception to the long established tradition that Trip was controlled by the Mechanics Institute, and that membership thereof should be the necessary qualification for a pass. Although the Institute had always been run by a committee of elected foremen and representative operatives, all of course GWR men, it was then considered by the trades unions that this friendly arrangement, which had worked so harmoniously for many years, was not in line with the changing times, and that the granting of passes should not be in the hands of what could be regarded as an outside body. As can well be imagined this was not a situation that could be settled at Swindon, and it had to go to the Board, at Paddington. One of the last decisions before nationalisation was that the Company would take it over, and this virtually sounded the death-knell of the Mechanics Institute in the form in which it had for so long been appreciated. Trip continued for many years afterwards, and still dominated the holiday affairs of Swindon. I well remember the astonishment of a young friend of ours who went to work in the town at how from May onwards the talk was of little else but Trip. It is sad to think that so old a tradition is now no more.

12
High Drama on the Cambrian

No writer of fiction or inventor of breath-taking film scenarios can ever have thought up a more thrilling or improbable sequence of convulsions in nature than that which actually occurred on the Oswestry–Aberystwyth line in the early evening of Sunday 21 June 1936. Even now the story is hardly believable but for the fact that the country folk who were the principal actors in this drama, told me in quiet dispassionate words about the amazing events of that Sunday evening; so, too, did the railwaymen who had to repair the damage wrought in so short a time. But first, the scene must be set for what could easily have been a tragedy, almost of Tay Bridge dimensions. The main line of the former Cambrian Railways, coming down from its summit in the Talerddig pass, enters the Severn Valley at Caersws, little more than a mile before reaching Moat Lane Junction, where the lengthy, meandering branch that leads down the Wye Valley to Builth Wells and Three Cocks Junction joins in. It was on the $4\frac{1}{2}$-mile section eastwards from Moat Lane to Newtown that Mother Nature struck so violently on that Sunday evening.

From the village of Caersws, where the main line first crosses the Severn, the river, here little more than a major mountain stream, follows a winding course, and it is crossed twice more within the next three miles. The scenery is beautiful and the valley is flanked on both sides by hills rising to around 1000ft, and from those on the south of the line there comes a tributary, the Dulais River, passing under the railway and joining the Severn immediately east of a halt named Scafell. This being Welsh border country the pronunciation is not the same as that of the mountain in the English Lake District but 'Scaffelth'. This halt then had a stationmistress, a Mrs Haynes, wife of a retired permanent way ganger, and they lived in the tiny station house, together with their daughter, a school teacher in Newtown, two miles to the east. That particular weekend had been terribly stormy, and on the Saturday amid thunderstorms of almost tropical violence the Severn burst its banks, and Newtown was flooded to an extent never previously experienced. But although the railway was, as yet, undamaged the conditions were such as to put everyone concerned on the alert. On Sunday the onslaught was renewed, and a day of thunder and torrential rain culminated about 6pm with a cloudburst in the hills to the south of the line, where the Dulais River has its source. This normally quiet mountain stream was soon a raging cataract, and fearing for the safety of the railway ex-Ganger Haynes and his daughter went out at the very height of the storm to keep watch.

East of the stone-arch bridge that carried the railway across the Dulais River the line runs for some distance on an embankment, and with all the surrounding fields flooded to a depth of about 5 or 6ft, and the waters surging around, their fears were of a possible washout of the embankment rather than a collapse of the bridge itself, which was a massive structure of 25ft span; amid the blinding rain they then saw that Dulais farmhouse just on the Newtown side of the river, was completely marooned and its ground floor rooms flooded to what looked like a depth of nearly 6ft. In the hopes of being able to give some help to the unfortunate people there Haynes and his daughter crossed the railway bridge, but they were hardly over when the utterly unbelievable happened. On the Scafell side of the river there was a group of huge elm trees, and in the terrific wind they were waving about like so many reeds. Suddenly, one of them was uprooted by the tremendous force of the rushing water, and by some extraordinary freak of the wind and the torrent it was borne downstream in a perfectly upright position, to crash into the railway bridge. It struck the parapet first, which was at once destroyed. The tree rebounded, but was then dragged underneath by the force of the current. Its passage ripped away the stonework at the crown of the arch and then the whole bridge collapsed.

Instantly, the situation changed from one of anxiety to deadly danger. It was not merely that there was a breach in the line nearly 60ft wide, but that the tree in its destructive passage underneath the arch had left the telegraph wires undamaged; with the block telegraph wires between Moat Lane Junction and Newtown still intact there was nothing to tell the signalmen at each end of that yawning gap over the Dulais River, in mid-section. Haynes, like the good railwayman he was, immediately thought of the up Mail, which by that time on a Sunday evening would already have left

Aberystwyth. It was due to call at Caersws at 7.57pm but the problem that faced Haynes and his daughter was that the breach in the line lay between them and the telephone in their cottage by Scafell halt. Across the gap the rails hung precariously in mid-air, but in such appalling weather conditions to attempt such a hazardous crossing was out of the question. A quick consultation between father and daughter decided upon a two-fold attempt to give warning of the danger. Haynes himself would attempt to wade across the flooded fields to reach the main road, about half a mile away, cross the river by the highway bridge, and try to get back to his home, and the telephone, by an equally watery way. It was not to be merely a matter of wading. The water was swirling and flowing in a way likely to sweep a man off his feet.

His daughter's share of this very brave affair was to walk two miles down the line to Newtown station, and give the alarm there. It was by no means certain that she would get through. In the prevailing conditions there could well have been another washout. The storm was, if anything, worse than ever, but in torrential rain, incessant thunder and lightning, and darkness almost of night this plucky girl set out on a tramp of nearly three quarters of an hour. Meanwhile her father, fortunately a fit man, although retired from railway service, was struggling through the floods to reach the main road. He had no sooner done this and crossed the bridge when this also was washed away. All this time the mail train was getting nearer. There were no signals at Scafell halt and the bridge was approached on a curve from a cutting. The speed of passenger trains at this point was usually about 55mph, and travelling thus in conditions of virtual nil-visibility the driver would never have been able to see the breach in the line in time to stop. But hasten as he tried to do it was hard going across those flooded fields back to the railway; when eventually he reached his cottage and telephoned Caersws he learned, to his great relief that his daughter had reached Newtown in time, and the mail train had been stopped.

With tragedy so narrowly averted one might have thought that Haynes would have been glad enough to relax, and get some dry clothes on, but he did not see it that way at all. Sunday night is proverbially a bad time for getting in touch with people in a hurry; nevertheless he managed to contact the Bridge Foreman at Caersws and to give him a detailed account of the way the bridge had collapsed, and how by subsequent damage to the abutments the breach in the line had been widened to nearly 60ft. Then, as if he had not done enough he went back to the main road to warn motorists of the broken bridge, and he continued to do so until 2am next morning. The Bridge Foreman at Caersws immediately contacted the Divisional Engineer at Oswestry, as such an occurrence as breaching of the main line needed immediate action – no waiting until staff assembled at the offices next morning. Calling in two senior assistants a meeting was held that same night; quick decisions were taken as to the form a temporary bridge would take, and before midnight the necessary materials had been ordered by wire.

Reflecting upon the events of that dramatic six hours up to midnight, on the evening of Sunday 21 June in 1936, one can indeed stand in admiration of the spirit, sense of high responsibility, and promptitude with which all concerned in turn acted. It is equally remarkable that when those three engineers sat down to scheme out the form the temporary replacement of the bridge should take that no one except ex-Ganger Haynes had actually *seen* what had happened, and that his evidence had been relayed by telephone to Oswestry via the Bridge Foreman at Caersws. Yet those senior engineers had no hesitation in placing complete confidence in the accuracy of his report. Nor was their confidence misplaced. The need for urgency was very great indeed, because in a fortnight's time the full summer service to the Cambrian coast was due to come into operation, with more trains and heavy week-end loading, characteristic of those holiday seasons between the two world wars. The prospect of packed Saturday holiday trains being stopped at Newtown for passengers to be conveyed thence to Caersws by bus did not bear thinking about. Of course there was no question of building a proper replacement of the bridge at once. The overriding need was to restore the railway link in the quickest possible temporary form, and this is what that late-night meeting of engineers at Oswestry decided upon.

It was hoped that second-hand girders would be available at one or other divisional headquarters of the GWR Chief Civil Engineer's department and the supporting piers were to be formed with clusters of stout timber piles. This intention was conveyed to the Bridge Foreman at Caersws when he had telephoned to advise Oswestry of the destruction of the original bridge. Acting with the utmost promptitude on that Sunday night the Bridge Foreman gathered his men together, loaded a train of material, including a pile driver, and was at Scafell by 5am on the Monday morning!

There was some difficulty in obtaining piles at such short notice, but by Tuesday morning this important part of the work began. But one cannot pass lightly over the situation on the morning after the storm, as it was seen and described to me by one of my friends who was on the job. The course of the Dulais River was one continuous trail of destruction. What remained of the railway bridge was lying out in the Severn; a filling station on the main road had been completely smashed up, and petrol pumps, a tea shelter, and other debris lay all over the surrounding fields. The highway authorities had also got a demolished bridge to replace. So far as the railway was concerned the abutment of the original bridge on the Newtown side had stood firm, but opposite, all had been completely washed away. The rails were still hanging in mid-air, and the track was firm enough for men to walk on. This was of no small help when the time came, later that week to lay the new temporary permanent way.

Even though faced with carrying the heaviest traffic of the year it was decided at once that the temporary bridge should be of single track only. There had been no points or signals at Scafell, and arrangements had to be made with other gangs to lay in crossover roads on each side of the Dulais River, and for temporary signalboxes to be installed. The block working between Newtown and Moat Lane Junction had to be altered, and provision made for single-line token working over the temporary bridge itself. A target time was set to have this work finished by the following Sunday, only one week after the washout. All this, including the provision of works trains from each side of the breach, and the inconvenience of having to terminate the regular passenger trains from each direction at Moat Lane and Newtown, involved a fairly hectic week of railway working. It was little more than routine though of an intense and complicatedly interlinked nature. The major task was the building of the temporary single-line bridge, and as if to make amends for the violence of the preceeding Sunday the weather, for the most part, was fine and dry, and photographs taken of the concluding stages showing the men shirt-sleeved and sweltering in hot sunshine were indeed a contrast to what had happened less than a week earlier.

The plan devised at that late-night meeting on the Sunday consisted of building two piers, one towards each side of the river, and each composed of a cluster of eight piles. They were arranged in two rows of four, with the rows at right angles to the line of railway. The piles themselves were massive timber baulks, 12in square in cross-section, and they were received on site in time for pile driving to begin on the Tuesday morning. They were driven down into the bed of the river, deeper and deeper, until at each blow of the pile driver they sank half an inch, or less. The engineers had, of course, full knowledge of the nature of the ground below the river bed, and were able to decide on this form of pier, as a temporary measure. After the tops of individual piers had been levelled off with each other, each row was surmounted by a horizontal member, known technically as a cap beam, and the uprights were then strongly cross-braced. They then had two immensely strong piers to support the temporary bridge. Whether they would have withstood a deluge such as that which demolished the abutment of the old bridge must remain unanswered. Fortunately they were not subjected to such a test. The final stage in preparation of the piers for the main girders of the temporary bridge was to fix two short horizontal timbers on each pier to support the girders.

The six second-hand girders, furnished by the Engineers' Department in response to that midnight wire, were of the plate type, each about 30ft long, but naturally not all of them could be used as actually received. The two main piers, made up of piles driven into the river bed, were approximately 25ft apart. Obviously in a temporary structure of this kind the joints between the girders had to be made immediately over the piers, for maximum support, and the two girders for the central span thus had to be cut down to size using an oxy-acetylene torch, no light task out in open country. With the two approach spans resting on firm ground at each end the temporary bridge thus had a length of 85ft. It did not have a solid deck. The track was to be carried on timber cross beams of the same cross-section as the piles in the main piers, 12in square, resting on the inner flanges of the main girders, and even when the track was laid one would look down straight through to the river below. Although the bridge gang from Caersws moved freely about on this exceedingly open framework, while the work was in progress things were made easier by laying a plank way along the suspended track of the old bridge. One of the two sets of rails that had remained hanging in mid-air after the washout was left in place for convenience during the week when the temporary bridge was being built. The work was finished and the line handed back to the Traffic Department at 4.30 pm on Sunday 28 June – a week all but a few hours after the original bridge had been destroyed. The temporary one was a rough and ready job, though immensely strong, but it was made subject to a permanent speed restriction of 5mph. How the new permanent bridge was built alongside, and in due course rolled into place on 15 November 1936 is another story.

13
The Great Western Tradition and its Influence

It might seem a little presumptious for an outsider, and a non-railwayman at that, to write about the traditions and eventual influence of so closely-knit, so much a family concern as the Great Western Railway. I cannot deny however that I have had close connections with it, and the Western Region, for the greater part of my life. For 59 years my home station has been on it; in the eight years when I was living in Central London Paddington was my nearest main line station, and at another time, when I was living elsewhere business took me frequently to the Westinghouse works at Chippenham. Over the years I have gathered a reputation for being a Great Western supporter, perhaps to the exclusion of most others. I shall always remember an occasion when I was to lecture to the railway society of Leeds University, and the Chairman introduced me thus: 'We all know Mr Nock is a GW fan. When he was at Imperial College, whenever his "Prof" wanted him they had to send a messenger to Paddington'! Perhaps the fact that out of my present tally of more than 100 full length books on railways 17 have been wholly concerned with the Great Western had led my Leeds friend to his facile, but quite wrong assumption. In my case that proportion of 14 per cent reflects rather upon the interest bestowed on the Great Western by enthusiasts in general, and here, after nearly 40 years of railway authorship I am just completing another.

Although in its long history there had been times when tradition looked like being overturned the Great Western had a large and diverse enough organisation to provide for a continuous succession of able men to fill its chief executive posts, without having to recruit from outside, and there were few indeed who had not been in the service of the Company throughout their working lives. Raymond Carpmael, who was Chief Engineer from 1930 to 1943, had his early training with the famous bridge and crane building firm of

161

Stothert & Pitt, of Bath, but joined the GWR as early as 1900, while C. B. Collett, Chief Mechanical Engineer from 1922, after studying at the City & Guilds (Engineering) College, in London, and serving a pupilage with a firm of eminent marine engineers, joined the GWR in the Locomotive Drawing Office in 1893, when he was 22 years of age. In 1900 he was appointed Assistant Manager in the Locomotive Works, and he remained a works man until he became Chief Mechanical Engineer. He was one of the very few chief officers who, on attaining that responsibility, had not moved around the railway in the course of his career, though the incidence of the first world war soon after he had been appointed Locomotive Works Manager, and his outstanding ability in production matters naturally kept him at headquarters.

Despite the distinction attained by the locomotives built at Swindon during his chieftainship one forms the impression that he was not in any way an engine designer himself, and had little inclination to aspire to be one. Possessed of a magnificent legacy from the Churchward era he would have been content to develop it to the extent of improved production methods, and reduced manufacturing and maintenance costs, and no more. But with Sir Felix Pole in the chair at Paddington there was no letting things remain in that quiescent state. In 1922 the first two Gresley Pacifics were built for the Great Northern Railway, at Doncaster, and in *The Railway Magazine* for February 1923 Cecil J. Allen wrote: '. . . now, at long last, a British type has appeared – granted, a much larger, heavier, and dimensionally more powerful engine – which will, I believe, give a Great Western 4–6–0 points and a beating. A bold claim, indeed, but, from my observations, one that is justifiable.' Knowing how avidly Pole read the railway literature of the day one can be fairly sure that those comments from Allen did not escape his attention, and although I have no documentary evidence to support it one can be fairly sure that Collett received a jog from Paddington, to do something about it! The idea of an enlarged Star was not new. In 1919 Churchward himself had the design of an enlarged boiler drawn out, with a maximum diameter of 6ft and a grate area of 30.3sq ft. Presumably the engine would have had larger cylinders also, but the total weight came out at $82\frac{1}{2}$ tons with a maximum axle load of $20\frac{1}{2}$ tons, and this the Civil Engineer would not accept. So this proposal for a super-Star came to nothing. In 1923, when a definite request came for a more powerful express passenger engine it was a case of making a compromise between the Star and the 1919 proposal; it was achieved by using the same length of barrel, 14ft 10in, but splitting the difference between the 5ft 6in maximum diameter of the Star and the 6ft 0in of 1919, and this held the total engine weight to $79\frac{3}{4}$ tons with a maximum axle load of $19\frac{3}{4}$ tons. Meanwhile the 1919 boiler had actually been built and fitted first to No 4700, and then to the eight further 47XX class 2–8–0s with 5ft 8in wheels built in 1921. With eight-coupled wheels the maximum axle load of the latter was 19.6 tons, and thus acceptable over what were classified as RED routes. So far as the new 4–6–0 was concerned, by some careful contriving it was found possible to increase the cylinder diameter from the 15in of the later Stars to 16in, and this one dimensional change put the tractive effort above that of the Gresley Pacific and everyone was happy.

So *Caerphilly Castle* emerged from Swindon in August 1923, and in the eyes of the beholders the thing that simply captivated attention was the restoration of the full pre-war livery, with all its glittering polished brass and copper work. One wonders if this also was the result of a jog from Paddington, because the austere, cost-conscious Collett had retained the wartime plain green painting with complete absence of all decorative touches on the Abbey series of Stars, turned out under his superintendence in 1922–3. With the Castles the Swindon tradition in engine style returned in all its glory, and everyone loved it. The test results from the *Caldicot Castle* were published in 1924. Then, they were so good, no one else believed them. When Collett was invited to read a paper to the World Power Conference held in that year it was an opportunity not to be missed. It would seem that the tests were carried out with the express purpose of providing data for that paper, because they were not completed until the end of March and the paper was presented in May. The fame of the Castles was established overnight, as it were, but little was appreciated at the time of how the engine was a rather hastily contrived compromise between Churchward's 1919 project, and what the Civil Engineer would accept.

The next prodding that Collett received came from within his own department, and not having the weight of Sir Felix Pole behind it bounced off him like a rubber ball. The prowess of the latest French compound locomotives was a live topic of discussion early in 1926, particularly as it was known that Sir Henry Fowler had received authority to build two large Pacifics embodying the latest developments of the de Glehn practice. Stanier, then Principal

Assistant to the CME, and Hawksworth, by that time Chief Draughtsman, got together, and having in mind the structural limitations still imposed by the GWR Chief Engineer, thought that by using compound propulsion they might be able to produce a more powerful engine than the Castle without exceeding the weight restrictions. To get in high pressure cylinders as large as 17in diameter they had to be placed ahead of the rear bogie wheels as on the Saint class, while by using a bogie wheelbase 1ft longer than standard, with its leading pair of wheels well forward, they could have low pressure cylinders 25in in diameter. The cylinder proportions were almost identical with those of the Bréville Pacifics introduced on the Northern Railway of France in 1922, and which were attracting much attention by their fine performances on the English boat trains, just as their Atlantic predecessors had done 20 years earlier. The compound would have been a considerably more powerful engine than a standard Castle, and having a tractive effort of 35,700 lb would have kept the Great Western well ahead of all others, despite the coming completion of *Lord Nelson* on the Southern, and the super-Pacifics of the LNER.

The days had changed completely from those of Churchward, who spent much time in the drawing office. He liked nothing better than to settle down at a drawing board where some new design was being worked out, gather around those who had interests involved and listen to all the arguments for and against. When the first 5ft 8in 2–8–0 No 4700 was being modified to have the large 1919 boiler designed for Churchward's super Star, a new feature was the use of direct outside steam pipes. Bill Pellow was making the drawings, and 'The Old Man' arrived at his board, accompanied by G. H. Burrows, who was then Chief Draughtsman, and he started to explain what they were doing. But Churchward immediately cut in: 'You shut up, Burrows, and let the young man tell me himself'. Pellow began to show how the outside steam pipes were being arranged, when Churchward said: 'Oh yes, I know; one of Stanier's gimcrack ideas!' 'Gimcrack' or not, the Old Man accepted it, and No 4700 as thus modified in 1921 became the first Great Western engine to have outside steam pipes.

As for the compound Castle, Collett apparently had no idea what his two topmost assistants were contriving early in 1926, but by the time enough had been done for the engine to be sketched out in outline Stanier thought it was time to show it to him. In contrast to Churchward as we have just seen, Collett hardly, if ever, went into the drawing office himself so an appointment had to be sought in his office. The outcome was vividly described to me by Hawksworth himself: 'We went in to see him, and in about five minutes we were out again!' And that was that. Tradition in Great Western locomotive design was not to be disturbed at that stage.

After he had assumed office as Chief Mechanical Engineer on New Year's Day 1922 Collett made a number of appointments that he clearly intended to remain for many years to come. When Collett himself became deputy CME Stanier had moved up to be Locomotive Works Manager, and in the autumn of 1922 he was further promoted to be Works Assistant to the CME. Many years later, when I was writing his biography Stanier told me how disturbed he was at the collateral appointments Collett made in 1922. The two men had been closely associated all through the difficult days of the first world war, and they had got on extremely well together; but when it came to the appointment of a successor to himself, as Locomotive Works Manager, they disagreed. Both were agreed on the outstanding ability of Hawksworth as an engine-designer, and upon the likelihood of him becoming a future CME. Stanier urged that he should have another spell in the works, following the tradition that on the GWR the locomotive 'bosses' should be all-rounders, which incidentally Collett was not! But with a view to him succeeding the veteran G. H. Burrows as Chief Draughtsman in a few years time Collett could not spare Hawksworth, and instead put in R. A. G. Hannington, an entirely felicitous appointment, even though his previous experience had been very largely at the divisional out-stations. Hannington was a delightful character, and led Swindon Works through an important and difficult period in its history with unqualified success.

The story of how the Locomotive Department was pitchforked into the production of the King class in a shipwreck hurry has been told before in many of its aspects; but after the furore had subsided and the brief alarm over the Midgham derailment had been weathered, the next thing to disturb the equanimity of the Collett regime was the departure of Stanier for the LMS, at the end of 1931. Though Collett let little escape through the dry impenetrable facade he usually presented to the world he was inwardly very upset at Stanier's going; he realised only too well how his Principal Assistant's delightful personality kept the wheels of the department well greased, and that everyone was happy. To succeed Stanier the Board appointed John Auld, who before the amalgamations of

1922 had been Chief Mechanical Engineer of the Barry Railway, and who since 1924 had been Docks & Personal Assistant to Collett. At the same time Hawksworth moved up to be Assistant to the CME. As John Auld was actually a year older than Collett, the appointments of 1932 virtually named Hawksworth as the next Chief Mechanical Engineer, although he had to wait nearly 10 years for the job.

Collett, with advancing years, took less and less interest in the day to day running of his great department, and yet he clung tenaciously to office. Nothing really new in the way of locomotives came out of Swindon after the Kings, and the only one slight departure from tradition, the Manor class 4–6–0, was badly proportioned and at first deficient in steaming power. Auld was left to carry on. He himself was anxious to retire, having passed the 65 mark in 1935. But Collett cajoled him into continuing, ostensibly so that he could say he (Collett) was not the oldest in the department. But while in the later 1930s, tradition, in the personality of the Chief Mechanical Engineer, was being carried almost to the point of stagnation so far as locomotive design practice was concerned, there was arising in the drawing office, and in its adjunct the testing section, a galaxy of young engineers who after the war were to give a new meaning to the phrase. 'Great Western tradition!' Before that it had been typical of the isolationism that Collett sought to enclose Swindon and its practice, by his deadly opposition to the Institution of Locomotive Engineers, which he once described as 'a lot of b—— commercial travellers'! And the London Divisional Locomotive Superintendent was under instructions regularly to attend their meetings and to report what was going on. Hawksworth, as much as anyone at Swindon realised where there was need for change, and some of his subsequent work has been described in Chapter 9 of this book.

When nationalisation came, in 1948, Great Western supporters were dismayed to see how thin was its representation on the British Transport Commission and The Railway Executive. While no company and its officers had contributed more wholeheartedly to the national war effort, through The Railway Executive Committee, the mere thought of permanent amalgamation under some politically imposed legislation, and the loss of their individuality, was just anathema to Great Western men. Of the General Managers who were members of the wartime REC Sir James Milne was by far the most senior, and he was the first choice for the Chairmanship of the Nationalised Railway Executive in 1948; but he turned it down, and so did Sir Allan Quartermaine when offered the position of Member of the Executive responsible for civil engineering and signalling. A sustained attempt was made to spread the new posts between the four Group companies, but the only Great Western officer to accept was David Blee, the former Chief Goods Manager, and not long afterwards it was said of him at Paddington that he had already forgotten he ever worked for the GWR. Of the strong men who were left, while it cannot be said that any of them seriously rocked the new BR boat, neither did they readily fall in with operational and engineering precepts that were notably different from their own and which they considered wholly inferior. Much of the work of coordination that was set in motion seemed like standardisation at the lowest level of previous achievement rather than aiming for better things.

On the locomotive side, while the Swindon organisation, which included the running, and all the footplate and shed staff within the responsibility of the Chief Mechanical Engineer, was different from those of the other Group railways, and due to be altered under BR, Hawksworth was spared the indignity of having his great department fragmented under his feet, as it were, as H. P. M. Beames had had to suffer at Crewe in 1923. But the fragmentation was fully discussed with K. J. Cook, his Principal Assistant, and all was ready for instant application the moment Hawksworth retired, at the end of 1949. Under R. A. Riddles the overriding influence in locomotive matters was solidly LMS, or so it seemed; but, with Hawksworth gone, the ex-LMS boffins at 'The Kremlin' – as Railway Executive headquarters at 222 Marylebone Road became sarcastically known – came up against some unexpectedly stout resistance from the new incumbent at Swindon, when the imposition of certain standards lower than those of the GWR were proposed.

Vacuum brakes became a major bone of contention. The Great Western had always worked at a vacuum of 25in, maintained while running by a crosshead pump; the others used 21in maintained by a small ejector blowing continuously. On trains like the West to North expresses, on which engines were changed at Shrewsbury, from GW to LMS, or vice versa, there was a long established routine for changing over from one degree of vacuum to the other. Southbound, the train would have been charged to 21in, and the Great Western engine coupling on would charge it to 25in and there would be no difficulty, and no action needed. Going north, the reservoir vacuum on each carriage had to be released by pulling a cord at footstep level, so that the train then operated at the lower vacuum. No difficulty had been experienced, even on through trains made up of part GW and part other companies' stock. There were other interchange points, such as Banbury, with trains from the GC line, and Oxford, where Southern railway locomotives took over through trains to Bournemouth, where the routine for changing vacuum was regularly performed without difficulty. But when new BR locomotive designs emanating from The Kremlin were in course of construction, and it was anticipated that they would be used throughout the network, including the Western Region, there was a definite prospect that the changeover between these and ex GWR locomotives would be likely to take place anywhere instead of at interchange points where the routine was well known, and a decree went forth that from then onwards the Western Region would use 21in of vacuum.

Much as this went against the grain with old Great Western locomotivemen, who felt they had got that extra in brake power in emergency and high speed, it was agreed that the locomotives could be altered very simply by resetting the vacuum relief valves. But a BR committee recommended that the brake gear on all ex-Great Western coaches should be modified to suit the lower vacuum, at an estimated cost of £350,000. As this would be a Regional expense to be incurred because of a lack of uniformity that had to be rectified, R. A. Riddles, Member of the Railway Executive for Mechanical & Electrical Engineering, sent the estimate to Keith Grand, Chief Regional Officer of the Western, leaving it for him to obtain authority from the Railway Executive for the expenditure to be incurred. Grand was horrified, and promptly asked K. J. Cook what it was all about. He replied that it could not be justified, and was, in fact, a complete waste of a lot of money. He pointed out that on the through train workings many Great Western coaches were running long mileages on 21in quite satisfactorily and had been for very many years; while it would mean a lower brake force this was no detriment in normal service. The only cases where it would result in a small increase in stopping distance would be an emergency application at very high speed; as no restoration of such trains was then contemplated there was no justification of any change. Riddles was furious!

In the summer of 1951 H. G. Ivatt of the LMS, the last of the old

Chief Mechanical Engineers was due to retire, and Riddles saw this as an opportunity to break down all the regional associations which had so far remained strong, despite nationalisation. The critical centres were clearly Derby, Doncaster and Swindon, so far as steam locomotive practice was concerned. After Bulleid went, in 1949, the Southern had been a province for electrical engineers, first Warder, and then Swift, though R. A. Smeddle, from Darlington, had a short spell on the Southern, as Assistant. But the big change round came after Ivatt's retirement on 30 June, 1951. So far as mechanical and electrical engineering was concerned the Eastern and North-Eastern Regions were combined, and J. F. Harrison, who had succeeded Peppercorn at Doncaster in 1950, went to Derby. K. J. Cook, much against his inclination, went to Doncaster, and Smeddle took the chair at Swindon. It was the most complete case of potential cross-breeding one could imagine, except, of course, that all three nominally came under the direction of Riddles at the Executive. I use the word 'nominally' with some deliberation, because I do not think any of those who planned the redistribution of the regional mechanical and electrical engineers quite anticipated what would happen in two out of the three cases. It could be summed up in the single phrase 'The Great Western Tradition.'

There was no more die-hard Geordie than Alfred Smeddle. His father had been Locomotive Running Superintendent of the North Eastern Railway, and during the first world war when Vincent Raven was away from Darlington, acting as Chief Superintendent of Woolwich Arsenal he acted as Assistant Chief Mechanical Engineer. His son, Alfred, from his apprenticeship at Darlington grew up deeply in the North Eastern tradition, with pictures of locomotives on which he had worked in his younger days. He rather horrified the natives by hanging them in Churchward's old office! But their consternation soon disappeared when they began to appreciate the nature of their new chief, his dynamic personality, and his qualities of leadership. In his younger days he had been much involved in dynamometer car testing from Darlington and he was at once much interested in the latest Swindon methods. Before he had gone north K. J. Cook had assured Grand that the former Great Western locomotives had been restored to their pre-war standards of maintenance, and that he was ready for major service accelerations; but as Grand discovered to his great annoyance, the locomotive department was not the only one he had to deal with.

The Locomotive Interchange Trials of 1948 had not shown the Great Western locomotives in their best light, and in the course of inter-regional conferences representatives of other interests had succeeded in convincing the rather defeatist Gilbert Matthews, who had been GWR Superintendent of the Line from January 1941, and held the office and title, that the locomotives were out-dated and incapable of showing their pre-war form. Smeddle had not long been at Swindon before he realised this was rubbish, and said so, to the delight of his staff. British Railways headquarters had decreed that to lessen maintenance costs smoke boxes of locomotives should be fitted with self-cleaning apparatus, in the form of wire mesh screens. Applied to certain notable types on other railways, without other adjustment, they had a disastrous effect on steaming; but at Swindon, at about the time Smeddle arrived, the testing section under Sam Ell was giving the most careful consideration to the fitting of these screens to both Castle and King class locomotives, and it was determined that some alteration to the draughting was necessary to compensate for the effect of the screens. Three engines were modified in 1952, two Kings and one Castle and won such golden opinions from the running staff as to convince Smeddle that they were even better than originally, without the screens, and from then on he threw his whole weight on the side of those who clamoured for service accelerations. At Smeddle's invitation I went to see No 6001 *King Edward VII* running on the stationary plant at Swindon, and one of those involved said delightedly of their new chief: 'He's more Great Western than any of us!'

Grand wanted to restore The Bristolian to its pre-war $1\frac{3}{4}$-hour schedule. Gilbert Matthews was still convinced that the engines were incapable of doing it. The magnificent results of the Brobdignagian test runs with No 6001, when a 25-coach train of 800 tons was worked at normal express train speed, and with good economy, cut no ice with him, despite Smeddle's confidence. At a critical meeting Grand lost his temper and exclaimed: 'Well, double-head the b—— thing, Gilbert!' Eventually a dynamometer car test run was arranged for 30 April 1954 and Grand himself rode on the footplate on the outward journey. Smeddle invited me to join them, and I was privileged to witness an immaculate piece of running, all the more so as we made an almost continuous round trip of 236 miles in 214 minutes, from Paddington to Paddington. In Bristol we stopped briefly at Dr Day's Bridge Junction to set down Mr Grand, and then for a little longer at Stapleton Road; but our total running time on the round trip was only 195 minutes, equal to an average speed of 72.6mph. The accelerated schedule came into force in June 1954, and as if to cast Gilbert Matthews's cold feet into his teeth – to mix the metaphors! – twice in the first week of running the up Bristolian arrived at Paddington nine minutes early.

Meanwhile Cook, having taken up the reins at Doncaster, was faced with a difficult and troubled situation. The Gresley three-cylinder Pacifics were still under something of a cloud from the failures experienced with them through overheated middle big-ends in the Interchange Trials of 1948; the mis-shapen Thompson Pacifics were already discredited, while the Peppercorns, though powerful engines, were disliked by the drivers for their alarmingly rough riding, and high coal consumption. Cook, although an outstanding workshop man, liked nothing better than to get out on the line, among the running people; although running was not then his responsibility his earlier training under Churchward and Hannington had made him much more of an all-rounder than many of his contemporaries on other regions. He found that construction practice at Doncaster where all the Gresley Pacifics were repaired was much more rough and ready than at Swindon, and that the motion of the three-cylinder engines had to be built with relatively large clearances in the pin-joints to avoid heating troubles. But this reacted in another way in that the two to one conjugated motion for the inside cylinder valve spindles developed an undue amount of slogger. This, in itself, did not lead to trouble, but it resulted in considerable over-running of the valves, and the inside-cylinder doing far more than its proportionate share of the total work.

In 1955 Kenneth Cook was President of the Institution of Locomotive Engineers, and in September of that year he titled his Presidential Address 'A Machine of Precision'. While those he had left behind at Swindon could succinctly be so described, those he had inherited at Doncaster were certainly not so. How he made them so is one of the heartwarming episodes in British locomotive history. At Swindon, when he was Assistant Manager of the Locomotive Works, the system of optical alignment of locomotive frames was set up, ensuring far greater accuracy in assembly than was possible by the methods then conventional. As a result the moving parts of the machinery did not require to have such liberal clearances in the bearings. It was said of Great Western locomotives that when the wear in pin joints and such like had reached the point at which they were scrapped, and renewal parts put in, they had just about reached the amount of clearance that some other railways provided when the bearings were new. In other words Swindon scrapped at the point where the others started! The apparatus installed at Swindon between the wars was of German manufacture, and was not available in the 1950s, but Cook found an English firm who could then supply similar equipment, and he installed it at Doncaster, and used it in repair of the Gresley Pacifics. The results were phenomenal. The ring and clanking that had been so characteristic of the three-cylinder engines with the conjugated valve motion disappeared completely. They ran with the quietness of well-oiled sewing machines, and troubles with overheated middle big-ends vanished. The Gresley Pacifics came into their own again as the premier express passenger locomotives of the East Coast route, and saw steam out in a blaze of glory, thanks to the influence of the Great Western.

Meanwhile a resolute attempt had been made to overturn and obliterate the Great Western tradition at Paddington. When Beeching put S. E. Raymond in as Chairman & General Manager of the Western Region one of his first crude acts was to have removed all the cherished pictures of the building of the Great Western Railway. It was probably true that the Western Region needed something of a shake-up. The financial position was not good, and passenger train running, except for a few crack trains, was poor. But there are more ways of effecting a shake-up than by antagonising everyone in sight, and bringing in another hard-bitten, humourless alien as his deputy. Apart from Beeching, to whom another WR General Manager always referred as 'the great and good Doctor' there was another harsh influence at 222 Marylebone Road, in the Vice-Chairman, Philip Shirley, whose one idea of making the railways pay would seem to have been to close everything down! I have already mentioned the incident of Raymond calling a meeting of chief officers on Cheltenham Gold Cup day; but his administration went a good deal further than tactical pinpricks to old traditions. Smeddle was still in office at Swindon when Raymond took over, but he was not well, suffering from an increasingly severe affliction, and he became more and more irritated by interference from the GM. It was a senior member of his staff who told of his return one day from a meeting at

Paddington. He told me how their greatly revered chief, tired and ill, at first did nothing but sit in his chair, the Chair of Churchward, Collett, and Hawksworth, and just consigned Raymond and his deputy to perdition in words that are quite unprintable here.

Fortunately for the men of the Western Raymond's stay was not long. He was called to higher things from which, eventually Barbara Castle dismissed him. In his place the Western got Gerard Fiennes. He has described himself as 'a hard-bitten operator'; that he may have been, but unlike his predecessor, who dashed round the railway trying to do everything himself, and upsetting all his senior officers in the process, Gerry Fiennes was a leader of men, who, while pointing the way clearly, left his very competent top management staff to do for themselves. He endeared himself to them all, and to the uniformed staff by his sense of humour, and the way he obviously enjoyed having the mickey taken out of him at social gatherings. He was appalled at the Western's poor record of passenger train timekeeping, and as a former operator worked strenuously to get that failing put right. Two of his top executive officers, T. Matthewson Dick (engineering) and H. M. Lattimer (operating) I had met first in my professional work, when they were both district officers at York, both as thorough-going North Eastern men as Alfred Smeddle. With Tommy Dick I became involved in marshalling yard modernisation, while he also gave me footplate passes to ride his engines in my spare time; with Bill Lattimer I was concerned with big resignalling schemes. And like Smeddle, when they both came south they so absorbed the Western atmosphere that they too became more GW than some of the natives – not to the extent in Tommy's case of losing his Geordie accent! As for Gerry Fiennes, he has confessed: '. . . while I was at Paddington I was Western over the ears'.

So indeed what is sometimes called the Great Western tradition envelopes most of those who come into contact with it, even those only distantly or not connected with the GWR. In its winter session of 1957–8 the Institution of Locomotive Engineers arranged a day visit to the Westinghouse works at Chippenham. Special restaurant car accommodation was provided for those travelling from London, and as Chief Draughtsman of the Company and a Member of the Institution I was one of those who met the President and his party at Paddington and travelled down with them. The Western Region signalled the occasion appropriately by putting on Castle class 4–6–0 No 7017 *G. J. Churchward* to haul the train. Maurice A.

Crane, a former Swindon pupil, and then London Manager of Beyer, Peacock & Co always organised these visits for the Institution, and although his railway experience after completion of his training at Swindon had been largely overseas he had always retained a great affection for the Works where he learned his job. We had reached the liqueur stage in the restaurant car and had passed Shrivenham when he stood up, and said in a loud voice: 'Gentlemen, you are now entering Wiltshire, and will shortly pass Swindon and its Works. You will now stand, as a token of your respect'! Amid much hearty laughter we did so, and had another drink on the strength of it. Here was another in whom the Great Western tradition had not lessened with the years.

Index

Associated Electrical Industries Co, 24

Baltimore & Ohio Railroad, 27, 29
Bincombe Tunnel, 136
Brake equipment: Armstrong development, 42; Direct Admission Valve, 44; leaking, 43; Sanders & Bolitho type, 41; vacuum automatic, 41 et seq, 167
Bridges, 28, 30

Coaches, 46-58
Control traffic, 124 et seq

Double-home working, 130-1
Dulais bridge washout, 154 et seq
Dutchman, the Flying, 39 et seq

Engineers: Armstrong, George, 12, 76; Armstrong, Joseph, 15; Armstrong, Joseph Junr, 41 et seq, 58, 75 et seq; Armstrong, R.J., 75; Auld, John, 165; Beames, H.P.M., 167; Blackall, A.T., 48, 60, 69; Bowen Cooke, C.J., 113; Brunel, I.K., 11, 21, 147; Burrows, G.H., 164; Carpmael, R., 161; Churchward, G.J., 22, 45, 48, 73 et seq, 164; Collett, C.B., 28 et seq, 109, 120, 162; Cook, K.J., 29, 121-2, 151, 167-9; Dean, W., 41, 75, 79; Deeley, R.M., 81; Dumas, C.K., 44, 115; Dymond, A.W.J., 29, 31, 112; Ell, S.O., 112 et seq; Ferreira, L.M.G., 61; Fowler, Sir

Henry, 163; Grierson, W.W., 22; Gooch, Sir Daniel, 21, 76, 147; Hall, F.C., 111, 121; Hannington, R.A.G., 29, 121, 165; Hawksworth, F.W., 29, 31, 57, 77, 84, 109 et seq, 164; Holden, James, 76; Inglis, Sir James, 18 et seq, 78; Innes, J.W., 58, 110; Insell, R.J., 61, 66; Inspectors, Loco, Running, 112; Ivatt, H.G., 168; Jacobs, C.M., 61, 66, 69; Lake, C.S., 88, 97; Lloyd, J.C., 28; Mattingley, F.C., 58, 110; Page, F.H.D., 72; Pearce, W.A., 64; Pearce, W.H., 81; Pellow, W., 111, 164; Quartermaine, Sir Allan, 167; Randle, H., 121; Riddles, R.A., 167-8; Roberts, C.T., 118 et seq; Smeddle, R.A., 169; Stanier, Sir W.A., 29, 67, 122, 163-5; Tew, G., 121; Willox, W.A., 91, 97; Wright, F.G., 80-1

Fishguard, 139
Flying Bomb attacks, 95, 109

GWR Magazine, 18

Holiday traffic, 91
Horses, shunting by, 13

Ireland, routes to, 20

'Kremlin', the, 167

Locomotive Engineering: Balancing, 30; Coal, quality, 113, 129; Compound Castle, 164; Dynamometer car tests, 118,

120; King class bogie, 31; Superheating, 113; Valve gears, model, 81; Walschaerts, gear, 81

Locomotives, individual: Caerphilly Castle, 163; Calcot Grange, 25; Caldicot Castle, 27, 115; Great Bear, The, 83, 114; Hurricane, 110; King Edward III, 114; King George V, 31, 51; King Henry VI, 59; Lady of Lynn, 120; Lord Nelson (Southern), 27; North Star, 83; Pendennis Castle, 27; Queen Matilda, 90; 2-8-0 No 4700, 85, 163
Locomotive Types: Armstrong 0-6-0, 15; Atbara 4-4-0, 79, 80; Badminton 4-4-0, 7, 79; Broad gauge 4-2-2, 9, 11, 58; Castle 4-6-0, 116 et seq; County class 4-6-0, 111; Hall 6959 series, 116, 136; King class 4-6-0, 31; Narrow gauge 2-4-0s, 11, 16; River class 2-4-0, 16; Saint class 4-6-0 30, 79; Star class 4-6-0, 30; USA, anglicised 4-6-2, 32
Locomotive Engineers, Institution of, 166

Magazine, the GWR, 18

Ocean traffic specials, 138 et seq
Operating, philosophy of, 91 et seq

Paddington: Christmas delays, 92-3; control coach, 126; rebuilding layout, 68; station closed, 1944, 95; traffic, 88

175

Index

Personalities: Aldington, C., 139; Allen, Cecil j., 24, 119, 162; Brocklebank, Sir Aubrey, 82; Churchill, Viscount, 21, 22, 78, 139; Crebbin, J.C., 82; Dewar, Major, 25, 95, 110; Doncaster, C., 6 *et seq*, 60; Fiennes, Gerard, 173; Gairns, J.F., 18, 89, 140; Grand, K.C., 168 *et seq;* Granet, Sir Guy, 29; Haynes, the family, 154 *et seq;* Hungerford, Ed, 27; Kay, J.A., 87 *et seq*, 109; Matthews, Gilbert, 126, 170; Milne, Sir James, 23, 25, 95, 166; Nicholls, R.H., 67; Pole, Sir Felix, 18 *et seq*, 52, 68, 162; Pole, Felix (Junr), 27, 32; Potter, Frank, 18; Pringle, Col Sir John, 67; Sekon, G.A., 87; Steer, Mrs W.,

100 *et seq*; Wilkinson, Sir Joseph, 21, 87; Willard, Daniel, 27, 32
Photography, early (Reading), 13

Race traffic, 143-5

Seat reservation, 125
Signalling: automatic train control, 67; early standards, 10; goods loops, 71; Newport, 66; power frames, 68; Reading 1940, 71; Slough, Bath Rd Jc, 63; Snow Hill, Birmingham, 61; Twisting of gantries, 70; Upper quadrant (Paddington), 62; Winchester, Cheesehill, 63
Slip coaches, 12, 34 *et seq*
Sonning Cutting, 8
Standardisation, 167 *et seq*
Stations: Cardiff General,

69; Newport (Mon), 66; Newton Abbot, 64; Paignton, 94; Reading, 6 *et seq*, 17, 132; Snow Hill (Birmingham), 61, 64; Swindon, 26, 32; Temple Meads (Bristol), 68
Strike, railway, 88
Swansea District Lines, 140
Swindon Works, 73 *et seq*, 146 *et seq*; Mechanics Institute, 147

Tradition (GW), overturning attempts that failed, 172
Trip, 147 *et seq*

Westinghouse Brake & Signal Co Ltd, 24, 26
Wivelscombe Rock Fall, 99 *et seq*

Zulu, the Northern, 13

176